C-3543   CAREER EXAMINATION SERIES

This is your
PASSBOOK for...

Senior Court Reporter

Test Preparation Study Guide
Questions & Answers

NATIONAL LEARNING CORPORATION®

COPYRIGHT NOTICE

This book is SOLELY intended for, is sold ONLY to, and its use is RESTRICTED to individual, bona fide applicants or candidates who qualify by virtue of having seriously filed applications for appropriate license, certificate, professional and/or promotional advancement, higher school matriculation, scholarship, or other legitimate requirements of education and/or governmental authorities.

This book is NOT intended for use, class instruction, tutoring, training, duplication, copying, reprinting, excerption, or adaptation, etc., by:

1) Other publishers
2) Proprietors and/or Instructors of "Coaching" and/or Preparatory Courses
3) Personnel and/or Training Divisions of commercial, industrial, and governmental organizations
4) Schools, colleges, or universities and/or their departments and staffs, including teachers and other personnel
5) Testing Agencies or Bureaus
6) Study groups which seek by the purchase of a single volume to copy and/or duplicate and/or adapt this material for use by the group as a whole without having purchased individual volumes for each of the members of the group
7) Et al.

Such persons would be in violation of appropriate Federal and State statutes.

PROVISION OF LICENSING AGREEMENTS – Recognized educational, commercial, industrial, and governmental institutions and organizations, and others legitimately engaged in educational pursuits, including training, testing, and measurement activities, may address request for a licensing agreement to the copyright owners, who will determine whether, and under what conditions, including fees and charges, the materials in this book may be used them. In other words, a licensing facility exists for the legitimate use of the material in this book on other than an individual basis. However, it is asseverated and affirmed here that the material in this book CANNOT be used without the receipt of the express permission of such a licensing agreement from the Publishers. Inquiries re licensing should be addressed to the company, attention rights and permissions department.

All rights reserved, including the right of reproduction in whole or in part, in any form or by any means, electronic or mechanical, including photocopying, recording, or by any information storage and retrieval system, without permission in writing from the Publisher.

Copyright © 2025 by
National Learning Corporation

212 Michael Drive, Syosset, NY 11791
(516) 921-8888 • www.passbooks.com
E-mail: info@passbooks.com

PASSBOOK® SERIES

THE *PASSBOOK® SERIES* has been created to prepare applicants and candidates for the ultimate academic battlefield – the examination room.

At some time in our lives, each and every one of us may be required to take an examination – for validation, matriculation, admission, qualification, registration, certification, or licensure.

Based on the assumption that every applicant or candidate has met the basic formal educational standards, has taken the required number of courses, and read the necessary texts, the *PASSBOOK® SERIES* furnishes the one special preparation which may assure passing with confidence, instead of failing with insecurity. Examination questions – together with answers – are furnished as the basic vehicle for study so that the mysteries of the examination and its compounding difficulties may be eliminated or diminished by a sure method.

This book is meant to help you pass your examination provided that you qualify and are serious in your objective.

The entire field is reviewed through the huge store of content information which is succinctly presented through a provocative and challenging approach – the question-and-answer method.

A climate of success is established by furnishing the correct answers at the end of each test.

You soon learn to recognize types of questions, forms of questions, and patterns of questioning. You may even begin to anticipate expected outcomes.

You perceive that many questions are repeated or adapted so that you can gain acute insights, which may enable you to score many sure points.

You learn how to confront new questions, or types of questions, and to attack them confidently and work out the correct answers.

You note objectives and emphases, and recognize pitfalls and dangers, so that you may make positive educational adjustments.

Moreover, you are kept fully informed in relation to new concepts, methods, practices, and directions in the field.

You discover that you are actually taking the examination all the time: you are preparing for the examination by "taking" an examination, not by reading extraneous and/or supererogatory textbooks.

In short, this PASSBOOK®, used directedly, should be an important factor in helping you to pass your test.

SENIOR COURT REPORTER

DUTIES
Senior Court Reporters are responsible for verbatim recording and transcribing testimony in formal and informal court settings such as trials, conferences, calendar calls, arraignments, and hearings. They may perform clerical and stenographic tasks directly related to court reporting work. Senior Court Reporters work in the Court of Claims, the Supreme Court, and those County Courts with 2 or more full-time County Court Judges or one full-time County Court Judge and combined annual filings of indictments and Supreme Court civil actions exceeding 650. They may also work in other courts during emergencies or in a difficult or protracted proceeding. They also perform clerical and other related duties.

SUBJECT OF EXAMINATION
The examination for Senior Court Reporter will consist of two components, a written test and dictation performance test. Candidates must obtain a passing score on each of the two components.

WRITTEN TEST
1. English grammar and usage, punctuation and sentence structure;
2. Spelling and vocabulary;
3. Legal and judicial procedures;
4. Medical and technical terminology.

Candidates will also be required to take a performance test consisting of taking and transcribing dictation of legal matter at speeds averaging from 175 to 200 words per minute. The performance test will simulate court proceedings. It will require candidates to take and transcribe an opening of counsel, averaging 175 words per minute for about three minutes; testimony involving four voices, including direct and cross examinations of witnesses, objection rulings, etc., averaging 200 words per minute for about eight minutes; and a judge's charge averaging 185 words per minute for about three minutes. Candidates must have an average of not more than five errors per hundred words dictated in order to obtain a passing mark of 70 in the performance test.

HOW TO TAKE A TEST

I. YOU MUST PASS AN EXAMINATION

A. *WHAT EVERY CANDIDATE SHOULD KNOW*

Examination applicants often ask us for help in preparing for the written test. What can I study in advance? What kinds of questions will be asked? How will the test be given? How will the papers be graded?

As an applicant for a civil service examination, you may be wondering about some of these things. Our purpose here is to suggest effective methods of advance study and to describe civil service examinations.

Your chances for success on this examination can be increased if you know how to prepare. Those "pre-examination jitters" can be reduced if you know what to expect. You can even experience an adventure in good citizenship if you know why civil service exams are given.

B. *WHY ARE CIVIL SERVICE EXAMINATIONS GIVEN?*

Civil service examinations are important to you in two ways. As a citizen, you want public jobs filled by employees who know how to do their work. As a job seeker, you want a fair chance to compete for that job on an equal footing with other candidates. The best-known means of accomplishing this two-fold goal is the competitive examination.

Exams are widely publicized throughout the nation. They may be administered for jobs in federal, state, city, municipal, town or village governments or agencies.

Any citizen may apply, with some limitations, such as the age or residence of applicants. Your experience and education may be reviewed to see whether you meet the requirements for the particular examination. When these requirements exist, they are reasonable and applied consistently to all applicants. Thus, a competitive examination may cause you some uneasiness now, but it is your privilege and safeguard.

C. *HOW ARE CIVIL SERVICE EXAMS DEVELOPED?*

Examinations are carefully written by trained technicians who are specialists in the field known as "psychological measurement," in consultation with recognized authorities in the field of work that the test will cover. These experts recommend the subject matter areas or skills to be tested; only those knowledges or skills important to your success on the job are included. The most reliable books and source materials available are used as references. Together, the experts and technicians judge the difficulty level of the questions.

Test technicians know how to phrase questions so that the problem is clearly stated. Their ethics do not permit "trick" or "catch" questions. Questions may have been tried out on sample groups, or subjected to statistical analysis, to determine their usefulness.

Written tests are often used in combination with performance tests, ratings of training and experience, and oral interviews. All of these measures combine to form the best-known means of finding the right person for the right job.

II. HOW TO PASS THE WRITTEN TEST

A. NATURE OF THE EXAMINATION

To prepare intelligently for civil service examinations, you should know how they differ from school examinations you have taken. In school you were assigned certain definite pages to read or subjects to cover. The examination questions were quite detailed and usually emphasized memory. Civil service exams, on the other hand, try to discover your present ability to perform the duties of a position, plus your potentiality to learn these duties. In other words, a civil service exam attempts to predict how successful you will be. Questions cover such a broad area that they cannot be as minute and detailed as school exam questions.

In the public service similar kinds of work, or positions, are grouped together in one "class." This process is known as *position-classification*. All the positions in a class are paid according to the salary range for that class. One class title covers all of these positions, and they are all tested by the same examination.

B. FOUR BASIC STEPS

1) Study the announcement

How, then, can you know what subjects to study? Our best answer is: "Learn as much as possible about the class of positions for which you've applied." The exam will test the knowledge, skills and abilities needed to do the work.

Your most valuable source of information about the position you want is the official exam announcement. This announcement lists the training and experience qualifications. Check these standards and apply only if you come reasonably close to meeting them.

The brief description of the position in the examination announcement offers some clues to the subjects which will be tested. Think about the job itself. Review the duties in your mind. Can you perform them, or are there some in which you are rusty? Fill in the blank spots in your preparation.

Many jurisdictions preview the written test in the exam announcement by including a section called "Knowledge and Abilities Required," "Scope of the Examination," or some similar heading. Here you will find out specifically what fields will be tested.

2) Review your own background

Once you learn in general what the position is all about, and what you need to know to do the work, ask yourself which subjects you already know fairly well and which need improvement. You may wonder whether to concentrate on improving your strong areas or on building some background in your fields of weakness. When the announcement has specified "some knowledge" or "considerable knowledge," or has used adjectives like "beginning principles of…" or "advanced … methods," you can get a clue as to the number and difficulty of questions to be asked in any given field. More questions, and hence broader coverage, would be included for those subjects which are more important in the work. Now weigh your strengths and weaknesses against the job requirements and prepare accordingly.

3) Determine the level of the position

Another way to tell how intensively you should prepare is to understand the level of the job for which you are applying. Is it the entering level? In other words, is this the position in which beginners in a field of work are hired? Or is it an intermediate or advanced level? Sometimes this is indicated by such words as "Junior" or "Senior" in the class title. Other jurisdictions use Roman numerals to designate the level – Clerk I, Clerk II, for example. The word "Supervisor" sometimes appears in the title. If the level is not indicated by the title, check the description of duties. Will you be working under very close supervision, or will you have responsibility for independent decisions in this work?

4) Choose appropriate study materials

Now that you know the subjects to be examined and the relative amount of each subject to be covered, you can choose suitable study materials. For beginning level jobs, or even advanced ones, if you have a pronounced weakness in some aspect of your training, read a modern, standard textbook in that field. Be sure it is up to date and has general coverage. Such books are normally available at your library, and the librarian will be glad to help you locate one. For entry-level positions, questions of appropriate difficulty are chosen – neither highly advanced questions, nor those too simple. Such questions require careful thought but not advanced training.

If the position for which you are applying is technical or advanced, you will read more advanced, specialized material. If you are already familiar with the basic principles of your field, elementary textbooks would waste your time. Concentrate on advanced textbooks and technical periodicals. Think through the concepts and review difficult problems in your field.

These are all general sources. You can get more ideas on your own initiative, following these leads. For example, training manuals and publications of the government agency which employs workers in your field can be useful, particularly for technical and professional positions. A letter or visit to the government department involved may result in more specific study suggestions, and certainly will provide you with a more definite idea of the exact nature of the position you are seeking.

III. KINDS OF TESTS

Tests are used for purposes other than measuring knowledge and ability to perform specified duties. For some positions, it is equally important to test ability to make adjustments to new situations or to profit from training. In others, basic mental abilities not dependent on information are essential. Questions which test these things may not appear as pertinent to the duties of the position as those which test for knowledge and information. Yet they are often highly important parts of a fair examination. For very general questions, it is almost impossible to help you direct your study efforts. What we can do is to point out some of the more common of these general abilities needed in public service positions and describe some typical questions.

1) General information

Broad, general information has been found useful for predicting job success in some kinds of work. This is tested in a variety of ways, from vocabulary lists to questions about current events. Basic background in some field of work, such as sociology or economics, may be sampled in a group of questions. Often these are principles which have become familiar to most persons through exposure rather than through formal training. It is difficult to advise you how to study for these questions; being alert to the world around you is our best suggestion.

2) Verbal ability

An example of an ability needed in many positions is verbal or language ability. Verbal ability is, in brief, the ability to use and understand words. Vocabulary and grammar tests are typical measures of this ability. Reading comprehension or paragraph interpretation questions are common in many kinds of civil service tests. You are given a paragraph of written material and asked to find its central meaning.

3) Numerical ability

Number skills can be tested by the familiar arithmetic problem, by checking paired lists of numbers to see which are alike and which are different, or by interpreting charts and graphs. In the latter test, a graph may be printed in the test booklet which you are asked to use as the basis for answering questions.

4) Observation

A popular test for law-enforcement positions is the observation test. A picture is shown to you for several minutes, then taken away. Questions about the picture test your ability to observe both details and larger elements.

5) Following directions

In many positions in the public service, the employee must be able to carry out written instructions dependably and accurately. You may be given a chart with several columns, each column listing a variety of information. The questions require you to carry out directions involving the information given in the chart.

6) Skills and aptitudes

Performance tests effectively measure some manual skills and aptitudes. When the skill is one in which you are trained, such as typing or shorthand, you can practice. These tests are often very much like those given in business school or high school courses. For many of the other skills and aptitudes, however, no short-time preparation can be made. Skills and abilities natural to you or that you have developed throughout your lifetime are being tested.

Many of the general questions just described provide all the data needed to answer the questions and ask you to use your reasoning ability to find the answers. Your best preparation for these tests, as well as for tests of facts and ideas, is to be at your physical and mental best. You, no doubt, have your own methods of getting into an exam-taking mood and keeping "in shape." The next section lists some ideas on this subject.

IV. KINDS OF QUESTIONS

Only rarely is the "essay" question, which you answer in narrative form, used in civil service tests. Civil service tests are usually of the short-answer type. Full instructions for answering these questions will be given to you at the examination. But in case this is your first experience with short-answer questions and separate answer sheets, here is what you need to know:

1) Multiple-choice Questions

Most popular of the short-answer questions is the "multiple choice" or "best answer" question. It can be used, for example, to test for factual knowledge, ability to solve problems or judgment in meeting situations found at work.

A multiple-choice question is normally one of three types—
- It can begin with an incomplete statement followed by several possible endings. You are to find the one ending which *best* completes the statement, although some of the others may not be entirely wrong.
- It can also be a complete statement in the form of a question which is answered by choosing one of the statements listed.

- It can be in the form of a problem – again you select the best answer.

Here is an example of a multiple-choice question with a discussion which should give you some clues as to the method for choosing the right answer:

When an employee has a complaint about his assignment, the action which will *best* help him overcome his difficulty is to
- A. discuss his difficulty with his coworkers
- B. take the problem to the head of the organization
- C. take the problem to the person who gave him the assignment
- D. say nothing to anyone about his complaint

In answering this question, you should study each of the choices to find which is best. Consider choice "A" – Certainly an employee may discuss his complaint with fellow employees, but no change or improvement can result, and the complaint remains unresolved. Choice "B" is a poor choice since the head of the organization probably does not know what assignment you have been given, and taking your problem to him is known as "going over the head" of the supervisor. The supervisor, or person who made the assignment, is the person who can clarify it or correct any injustice. Choice "C" is, therefore, correct. To say nothing, as in choice "D," is unwise. Supervisors have and interest in knowing the problems employees are facing, and the employee is seeking a solution to his problem.

2) True/False Questions

The "true/false" or "right/wrong" form of question is sometimes used. Here a complete statement is given. Your job is to decide whether the statement is right or wrong.

SAMPLE: A roaming cell-phone call to a nearby city costs less than a non-roaming call to a distant city.

This statement is wrong, or false, since roaming calls are more expensive.

This is not a complete list of all possible question forms, although most of the others are variations of these common types. You will always get complete directions for answering questions. Be sure you understand *how* to mark your answers – ask questions until you do.

V. RECORDING YOUR ANSWERS

Computer terminals are used more and more today for many different kinds of exams.

For an examination with very few applicants, you may be told to record your answers in the test booklet itself. Separate answer sheets are much more common. If this separate answer sheet is to be scored by machine – and this is often the case – it is highly important that you mark your answers correctly in order to get credit.

An electronic scoring machine is often used in civil service offices because of the speed with which papers can be scored. Machine-scored answer sheets must be marked with a pencil, which will be given to you. This pencil has a high graphite content which responds to the electronic scoring machine. As a matter of fact, stray dots may register as answers, so do not let your pencil rest on the answer sheet while you are pondering the correct answer. Also, if your pencil lead breaks or is otherwise defective, ask for another.

Since the answer sheet will be dropped in a slot in the scoring machine, be careful not to bend the corners or get the paper crumpled.

The answer sheet normally has five vertical columns of numbers, with 30 numbers to a column. These numbers correspond to the question numbers in your test booklet. After each number, going across the page are four or five pairs of dotted lines. These short dotted lines have small letters or numbers above them. The first two pairs may also have a "T" or "F" above the letters. This indicates that the first two pairs only are to be used if the questions are of the true-false type. If the questions are multiple choice, disregard the "T" and "F" and pay attention only to the small letters or numbers.

Answer your questions in the manner of the sample that follows:

32. The largest city in the United States is
    A. Washington, D.C.
    B. New York City
    C. Chicago
    D. Detroit
    E. San Francisco

1) Choose the answer you think is best. (New York City is the largest, so "B" is correct.)
2) Find the row of dotted lines numbered the same as the question you are answering. (Find row number 32)
3) Find the pair of dotted lines corresponding to the answer. (Find the pair of lines under the mark "B.")
4) Make a solid black mark between the dotted lines.

VI. BEFORE THE TEST

Common sense will help you find procedures to follow to get ready for an examination. Too many of us, however, overlook these sensible measures. Indeed, nervousness and fatigue have been found to be the most serious reasons why applicants fail to do their best on civil service tests. Here is a list of reminders:

- Begin your preparation early – Don't wait until the last minute to go scurrying around for books and materials or to find out what the position is all about.
- Prepare continuously – An hour a night for a week is better than an all-night cram session. This has been definitely established. What is more, a night a week for a month will return better dividends than crowding your study into a shorter period of time.
- Locate the place of the exam – You have been sent a notice telling you when and where to report for the examination. If the location is in a different town or otherwise unfamiliar to you, it would be well to inquire the best route and learn something about the building.
- Relax the night before the test – Allow your mind to rest. Do not study at all that night. Plan some mild recreation or diversion; then go to bed early and get a good night's sleep.
- Get up early enough to make a leisurely trip to the place for the test – This way unforeseen events, traffic snarls, unfamiliar buildings, etc. will not upset you.
- Dress comfortably – A written test is not a fashion show. You will be known by number and not by name, so wear something comfortable.

- Leave excess paraphernalia at home – Shopping bags and odd bundles will get in your way. You need bring only the items mentioned in the official notice you received; usually everything you need is provided. Do not bring reference books to the exam. They will only confuse those last minutes and be taken away from you when in the test room.
- Arrive somewhat ahead of time – If because of transportation schedules you must get there very early, bring a newspaper or magazine to take your mind off yourself while waiting.
- Locate the examination room – When you have found the proper room, you will be directed to the seat or part of the room where you will sit. Sometimes you are given a sheet of instructions to read while you are waiting. Do not fill out any forms until you are told to do so; just read them and be prepared.
- Relax and prepare to listen to the instructions
- If you have any physical problem that may keep you from doing your best, be sure to tell the test administrator. If you are sick or in poor health, you really cannot do your best on the exam. You can come back and take the test some other time.

VII. AT THE TEST

The day of the test is here and you have the test booklet in your hand. The temptation to get going is very strong. Caution! There is more to success than knowing the right answers. You must know how to identify your papers and understand variations in the type of short-answer question used in this particular examination. Follow these suggestions for maximum results from your efforts:

1) Cooperate with the monitor

The test administrator has a duty to create a situation in which you can be as much at ease as possible. He will give instructions, tell you when to begin, check to see that you are marking your answer sheet correctly, and so on. He is not there to guard you, although he will see that your competitors do not take unfair advantage. He wants to help you do your best.

2) Listen to all instructions

Don't jump the gun! Wait until you understand all directions. In most civil service tests you get more time than you need to answer the questions. So don't be in a hurry. Read each word of instructions until you clearly understand the meaning. Study the examples, listen to all announcements and follow directions. Ask questions if you do not understand what to do.

3) Identify your papers

Civil service exams are usually identified by number only. You will be assigned a number; you must not put your name on your test papers. Be sure to copy your number correctly. Since more than one exam may be given, copy your exact examination title.

4) Plan your time

Unless you are told that a test is a "speed" or "rate of work" test, speed itself is usually not important. Time enough to answer all the questions will be provided, but this does not mean that you have all day. An overall time limit has been set. Divide the total time (in minutes) by the number of questions to determine the approximate time you have for each question.

5) Do not linger over difficult questions

If you come across a difficult question, mark it with a paper clip (useful to have along) and come back to it when you have been through the booklet. One caution if you do this – be sure to skip a number on your answer sheet as well. Check often to be sure that you have not lost your place and that you are marking in the row numbered the same as the question you are answering.

6) Read the questions

Be sure you know what the question asks! Many capable people are unsuccessful because they failed to *read* the questions correctly.

7) Answer all questions

Unless you have been instructed that a penalty will be deducted for incorrect answers, it is better to guess than to omit a question.

8) Speed tests

It is often better NOT to guess on speed tests. It has been found that on timed tests people are tempted to spend the last few seconds before time is called in marking answers at random – without even reading them – in the hope of picking up a few extra points. To discourage this practice, the instructions may warn you that your score will be "corrected" for guessing. That is, a penalty will be applied. The incorrect answers will be deducted from the correct ones, or some other penalty formula will be used.

9) Review your answers

If you finish before time is called, go back to the questions you guessed or omitted to give them further thought. Review other answers if you have time.

10) Return your test materials

If you are ready to leave before others have finished or time is called, take ALL your materials to the monitor and leave quietly. Never take any test material with you. The monitor can discover whose papers are not complete, and taking a test booklet may be grounds for disqualification.

VIII. EXAMINATION TECHNIQUES

1) Read the general instructions carefully. These are usually printed on the first page of the exam booklet. As a rule, these instructions refer to the timing of the examination; the fact that you should not start work until the signal and must stop work at a signal, etc. If there are any *special* instructions, such as a choice of questions to be answered, make sure that you note this instruction carefully.

2) When you are ready to start work on the examination, that is as soon as the signal has been given, read the instructions to each question booklet, underline any key words or phrases, such as *least, best, outline, describe* and the like. In this way you will tend to answer as requested rather than discover on reviewing your paper that you *listed without describing*, that you selected the *worst* choice rather than the *best* choice, etc.

3) If the examination is of the objective or multiple-choice type – that is, each question will also give a series of possible answers: A, B, C or D, and you are called upon to select the best answer and write the letter next to that answer on your answer paper – it is advisable to start answering each question in turn. There may be anywhere from 50 to 100 such questions in the three or four hours allotted and you can see how much time would be taken if you read through all the questions before beginning to answer any. Furthermore, if you come across a question or group of questions which you know would be difficult to answer, it would undoubtedly affect your handling of all the other questions.

4) If the examination is of the essay type and contains but a few questions, it is a moot point as to whether you should read all the questions before starting to answer any one. Of course, if you are given a choice – say five out of seven and the like – then it is essential to read all the questions so you can eliminate the two that are most difficult. If, however, you are asked to answer all the questions, there may be danger in trying to answer the easiest one first because you may find that you will spend too much time on it. The best technique is to answer the first question, then proceed to the second, etc.

5) Time your answers. Before the exam begins, write down the time it started, then add the time allowed for the examination and write down the time it must be completed, then divide the time available somewhat as follows:
    - If 3-1/2 hours are allowed, that would be 210 minutes. If you have 80 objective-type questions, that would be an average of 2-1/2 minutes per question. Allow yourself no more than 2 minutes per question, or a total of 160 minutes, which will permit about 50 minutes to review.
    - If for the time allotment of 210 minutes there are 7 essay questions to answer, that would average about 30 minutes a question. Give yourself only 25 minutes per question so that you have about 35 minutes to review.

6) The most important instruction is to *read each question* and make sure you know what is wanted. The second most important instruction is to *time yourself properly* so that you answer every question. The third most important instruction is to *answer every question*. Guess if you have to but include something for each question. Remember that you will receive no credit for a blank and will probably receive some credit if you write something in answer to an essay question. If you guess a letter – say "B" for a multiple-choice question – you may have guessed right. If you leave a blank as an answer to a multiple-choice question, the examiners may respect your feelings but it will not add a point to your score. Some exams may penalize you for wrong answers, so in such cases *only*, you may not want to guess unless you have some basis for your answer.

7) Suggestions
    a. Objective-type questions
        1. Examine the question booklet for proper sequence of pages and questions
        2. Read all instructions carefully
        3. Skip any question which seems too difficult; return to it after all other questions have been answered
        4. Apportion your time properly; do not spend too much time on any single question or group of questions

5. Note and underline key words – *all, most, fewest, least, best, worst, same, opposite*, etc.
6. Pay particular attention to negatives
7. Note unusual option, e.g., unduly long, short, complex, different or similar in content to the body of the question
8. Observe the use of "hedging" words – *probably, may, most likely*, etc.
9. Make sure that your answer is put next to the same number as the question
10. Do not second-guess unless you have good reason to believe the second answer is definitely more correct
11. Cross out original answer if you decide another answer is more accurate; do not erase until you are ready to hand your paper in
12. Answer all questions; guess unless instructed otherwise
13. Leave time for review

   b. Essay questions
     1. Read each question carefully
     2. Determine exactly what is wanted. Underline key words or phrases.
     3. Decide on outline or paragraph answer
     4. Include many different points and elements unless asked to develop any one or two points or elements
     5. Show impartiality by giving pros and cons unless directed to select one side only
     6. Make and write down any assumptions you find necessary to answer the questions
     7. Watch your English, grammar, punctuation and choice of words
     8. Time your answers; don't crowd material

8) Answering the essay question

Most essay questions can be answered by framing the specific response around several key words or ideas. Here are a few such key words or ideas:

M's: manpower, materials, methods, money, management
P's: purpose, program, policy, plan, procedure, practice, problems, pitfalls, personnel, public relations
   a. Six basic steps in handling problems:
     1. Preliminary plan and background development
     2. Collect information, data and facts
     3. Analyze and interpret information, data and facts
     4. Analyze and develop solutions as well as make recommendations
     5. Prepare report and sell recommendations
     6. Install recommendations and follow up effectiveness

   b. Pitfalls to avoid
     1. *Taking things for granted* – A statement of the situation does not necessarily imply that each of the elements is necessarily true; for example, a complaint may be invalid and biased so that all that can be taken for granted is that a complaint has been registered

2. *Considering only one side of a situation* – Wherever possible, indicate several alternatives and then point out the reasons you selected the best one
3. *Failing to indicate follow up* – Whenever your answer indicates action on your part, make certain that you will take proper follow-up action to see how successful your recommendations, procedures or actions turn out to be
4. *Taking too long in answering any single question* – Remember to time your answers properly

IX. AFTER THE TEST

Scoring procedures differ in detail among civil service jurisdictions although the general principles are the same. Whether the papers are hand-scored or graded by machine we have described, they are nearly always graded by number. That is, the person who marks the paper knows only the number – never the name – of the applicant. Not until all the papers have been graded will they be matched with names. If other tests, such as training and experience or oral interview ratings have been given, scores will be combined. Different parts of the examination usually have different weights. For example, the written test might count 60 percent of the final grade, and a rating of training and experience 40 percent. In many jurisdictions, veterans will have a certain number of points added to their grades.

After the final grade has been determined, the names are placed in grade order and an eligible list is established. There are various methods for resolving ties between those who get the same final grade – probably the most common is to place first the name of the person whose application was received first. Job offers are made from the eligible list in the order the names appear on it. You will be notified of your grade and your rank as soon as all these computations have been made. This will be done as rapidly as possible.

People who are found to meet the requirements in the announcement are called "eligibles." Their names are put on a list of eligible candidates. An eligible's chances of getting a job depend on how high he stands on this list and how fast agencies are filling jobs from the list.

When a job is to be filled from a list of eligibles, the agency asks for the names of people on the list of eligibles for that job. When the civil service commission receives this request, it sends to the agency the names of the three people highest on this list. Or, if the job to be filled has specialized requirements, the office sends the agency the names of the top three persons who meet these requirements from the general list.

The appointing officer makes a choice from among the three people whose names were sent to him. If the selected person accepts the appointment, the names of the others are put back on the list to be considered for future openings.

That is the rule in hiring from all kinds of eligible lists, whether they are for typist, carpenter, chemist, or something else. For every vacancy, the appointing officer has his choice of any one of the top three eligibles on the list. This explains why the person whose name is on top of the list sometimes does not get an appointment when some of the persons lower on the list do. If the appointing officer chooses the second or third eligible, the No. 1 eligible does not get a job at once, but stays on the list until he is appointed or the list is terminated.

X. HOW TO PASS THE INTERVIEW TEST

The examination for which you applied requires an oral interview test. You have already taken the written test and you are now being called for the interview test – the final part of the formal examination.

You may think that it is not possible to prepare for an interview test and that there are no procedures to follow during an interview. Our purpose is to point out some things you can do in advance that will help you and some good rules to follow and pitfalls to avoid while you are being interviewed.

What is an interview supposed to test?

The written examination is designed to test the technical knowledge and competence of the candidate; the oral is designed to evaluate intangible qualities, not readily measured otherwise, and to establish a list showing the relative fitness of each candidate – as measured against his competitors – for the position sought. Scoring is not on the basis of "right" and "wrong," but on a sliding scale of values ranging from "not passable" to "outstanding." As a matter of fact, it is possible to achieve a relatively low score without a single "incorrect" answer because of evident weakness in the qualities being measured.

Occasionally, an examination may consist entirely of an oral test – either an individual or a group oral. In such cases, information is sought concerning the technical knowledges and abilities of the candidate, since there has been no written examination for this purpose. More commonly, however, an oral test is used to supplement a written examination.

Who conducts interviews?

The composition of oral boards varies among different jurisdictions. In nearly all, a representative of the personnel department serves as chairman. One of the members of the board may be a representative of the department in which the candidate would work. In some cases, "outside experts" are used, and, frequently, a businessman or some other representative of the general public is asked to serve. Labor and management or other special groups may be represented. The aim is to secure the services of experts in the appropriate field.

However the board is composed, it is a good idea (and not at all improper or unethical) to ascertain in advance of the interview who the members are and what groups they represent. When you are introduced to them, you will have some idea of their backgrounds and interests, and at least you will not stutter and stammer over their names.

What should be done before the interview?

While knowledge about the board members is useful and takes some of the surprise element out of the interview, there is other preparation which is more substantive. It *is* possible to prepare for an oral interview – in several ways:

1) Keep a copy of your application and review it carefully before the interview

This may be the only document before the oral board, and the starting point of the interview. Know what education and experience you have listed there, and the sequence and dates of all of it. Sometimes the board will ask you to review the highlights of your experience for them; you should not have to hem and haw doing it.

2) Study the class specification and the examination announcement

Usually, the oral board has one or both of these to guide them. The qualities, characteristics or knowledges required by the position sought are stated in these documents. They offer valuable clues as to the nature of the oral interview. For example, if the job involves supervisory responsibilities, the announcement will usually indicate that knowledge of modern supervisory methods and the qualifications of the candidate as a supervisor will be tested. If so, you can expect such questions, frequently in the form of a hypothetical situation which you are expected to solve. NEVER go into an oral without knowledge of the duties and responsibilities of the job you seek.

3) Think through each qualification required

Try to visualize the kind of questions you would ask if you were a board member. How well could you answer them? Try especially to appraise your own knowledge and background in each area, *measured against the job sought*, and identify any areas in which you are weak. Be critical and realistic – do not flatter yourself.

4) Do some general reading in areas in which you feel you may be weak

For example, if the job involves supervision and your past experience has NOT, some general reading in supervisory methods and practices, particularly in the field of human relations, might be useful. Do NOT study agency procedures or detailed manuals. The oral board will be testing your understanding and capacity, not your memory.

5) Get a good night's sleep and watch your general health and mental attitude

You will want a clear head at the interview. Take care of a cold or any other minor ailment, and of course, no hangovers.

What should be done on the day of the interview?

Now comes the day of the interview itself. Give yourself plenty of time to get there. Plan to arrive somewhat ahead of the scheduled time, particularly if your appointment is in the fore part of the day. If a previous candidate fails to appear, the board might be ready for you a bit early. By early afternoon an oral board is almost invariably behind schedule if there are many candidates, and you may have to wait. Take along a book or magazine to read, or your application to review, but leave any extraneous material in the waiting room when you go in for your interview. In any event, relax and compose yourself.

The matter of dress is important. The board is forming impressions about you – from your experience, your manners, your attitude, and your appearance. Give your personal appearance careful attention. Dress your best, but not your flashiest. Choose conservative, appropriate clothing, and be sure it is immaculate. This is a business interview, and your appearance should indicate that you regard it as such. Besides, being well groomed and properly dressed will help boost your confidence.

Sooner or later, someone will call your name and escort you into the interview room. *This is it.* From here on you are on your own. It is too late for any more preparation. But remember, you asked for this opportunity to prove your fitness, and you are here because your request was granted.

What happens when you go in?

The usual sequence of events will be as follows: The clerk (who is often the board stenographer) will introduce you to the chairman of the oral board, who will introduce you to the other members of the board. Acknowledge the introductions before you sit down. Do not be surprised if you find a microphone facing you or a stenotypist sitting by. Oral interviews are usually recorded in the event of an appeal or other review.

Usually the chairman of the board will open the interview by reviewing the highlights of your education and work experience from your application – primarily for the benefit of the other members of the board, as well as to get the material into the record. Do not interrupt or comment unless there is an error or significant misinterpretation; if that is the case, do not hesitate. But do not quibble about insignificant matters. Also, he will usually ask you some question about your education, experience or your present job – partly to get you to start talking and to establish the interviewing "rapport." He may start the actual questioning, or turn it over to one of the other members. Frequently, each member undertakes the questioning on a particular area, one in which he is perhaps most competent, so you can expect each member to participate in the examination. Because time is limited, you may also expect some rather abrupt switches in the direction the questioning takes, so do not be upset by it. Normally, a board member will not pursue a single line of questioning unless he discovers a particular strength or weakness.

After each member has participated, the chairman will usually ask whether any member has any further questions, then will ask you if you have anything you wish to add. Unless you are expecting this question, it may floor you. Worse, it may start you off on an extended, extemporaneous speech. The board is not usually seeking more information. The question is principally to offer you a last opportunity to present further qualifications or to indicate that you have nothing to add. So, if you feel that a significant qualification or characteristic has been overlooked, it is proper to point it out in a sentence or so. Do not compliment the board on the thoroughness of their examination – they have been sketchy, and you know it. If you wish, merely say, "No thank you, I have nothing further to add." This is a point where you can "talk yourself out" of a good impression or fail to present an important bit of information. Remember, *you close the interview yourself*.

The chairman will then say, "That is all, Mr. _____, thank you." Do not be startled; the interview is over, and quicker than you think. Thank him, gather your belongings and take your leave. Save your sigh of relief for the other side of the door.

How to put your best foot forward

Throughout this entire process, you may feel that the board individually and collectively is trying to pierce your defenses, seek out your hidden weaknesses and embarrass and confuse you. Actually, this is not true. They are obliged to make an appraisal of your qualifications for the job you are seeking, and they want to see you in your best light. Remember, they must interview all candidates and a non-cooperative candidate may become a failure in spite of their best efforts to bring out his qualifications. Here are 15 suggestions that will help you:

1) Be natural – Keep your attitude confident, not cocky

If you are not confident that you can do the job, do not expect the board to be. Do not apologize for your weaknesses, try to bring out your strong points. The board is interested in a positive, not negative, presentation. Cockiness will antagonize any board member and make him wonder if you are covering up a weakness by a false show of strength.

2) Get comfortable, but don't lounge or sprawl

Sit erectly but not stiffly. A careless posture may lead the board to conclude that you are careless in other things, or at least that you are not impressed by the importance of the occasion. Either conclusion is natural, even if incorrect. Do not fuss with your clothing, a pencil or an ashtray. Your hands may occasionally be useful to emphasize a point; do not let them become a point of distraction.

3) Do not wisecrack or make small talk

This is a serious situation, and your attitude should show that you consider it as such. Further, the time of the board is limited – they do not want to waste it, and neither should you.

4) Do not exaggerate your experience or abilities

In the first place, from information in the application or other interviews and sources, the board may know more about you than you think. Secondly, you probably will not get away with it. An experienced board is rather adept at spotting such a situation, so do not take the chance.

5) If you know a board member, do not make a point of it, yet do not hide it

Certainly you are not fooling him, and probably not the other members of the board. Do not try to take advantage of your acquaintanceship – it will probably do you little good.

6) Do not dominate the interview

Let the board do that. They will give you the clues – do not assume that you have to do all the talking. Realize that the board has a number of questions to ask you, and do not try to take up all the interview time by showing off your extensive knowledge of the answer to the first one.

7) Be attentive

You only have 20 minutes or so, and you should keep your attention at its sharpest throughout. When a member is addressing a problem or question to you, give him your undivided attention. Address your reply principally to him, but do not exclude the other board members.

8) Do not interrupt

A board member may be stating a problem for you to analyze. He will ask you a question when the time comes. Let him state the problem, and wait for the question.

9) Make sure you understand the question

Do not try to answer until you are sure what the question is. If it is not clear, restate it in your own words or ask the board member to clarify it for you. However, do not haggle about minor elements.

10) Reply promptly but not hastily

A common entry on oral board rating sheets is "candidate responded readily," or "candidate hesitated in replies." Respond as promptly and quickly as you can, but do not jump to a hasty, ill-considered answer.

11) Do not be peremptory in your answers

A brief answer is proper – but do not fire your answer back. That is a losing game from your point of view. The board member can probably ask questions much faster than you can answer them.

12) Do not try to create the answer you think the board member wants

He is interested in what kind of mind you have and how it works – not in playing games. Furthermore, he can usually spot this practice and will actually grade you down on it.

13) Do not switch sides in your reply merely to agree with a board member

Frequently, a member will take a contrary position merely to draw you out and to see if you are willing and able to defend your point of view. Do not start a debate, yet do not surrender a good position. If a position is worth taking, it is worth defending.

14) Do not be afraid to admit an error in judgment if you are shown to be wrong

The board knows that you are forced to reply without any opportunity for careful consideration. Your answer may be demonstrably wrong. If so, admit it and get on with the interview.

15) Do not dwell at length on your present job

The opening question may relate to your present assignment. Answer the question but do not go into an extended discussion. You are being examined for a *new* job, not your present one. As a matter of fact, try to phrase ALL your answers in terms of the job for which you are being examined.

Basis of Rating

Probably you will forget most of these "do's" and "don'ts" when you walk into the oral interview room. Even remembering them all will not ensure you a passing grade. Perhaps you did not have the qualifications in the first place. But remembering them will help you to put your best foot forward, without treading on the toes of the board members.

Rumor and popular opinion to the contrary notwithstanding, an oral board wants you to make the best appearance possible. They know you are under pressure – but they also want to see how you respond to it as a guide to what your reaction would be under the pressures of the job you seek. They will be influenced by the degree of poise you display, the personal traits you show and the manner in which you respond.

ABOUT THIS BOOK

This book contains tests divided into Examination Sections. Go through each test, answering every question in the margin. We have also attached a sample answer sheet at the back of the book that can be removed and used. At the end of each test look at the answer key and check your answers. On the ones you got wrong, look at the right answer choice and learn. Do not fill in the answers first. Do not memorize the questions and answers, but understand the answer and principles involved. On your test, the questions will likely be different from the samples. Questions are changed and new ones added. If you understand these past questions you should have success with any changes that arise. Tests may consist of several types of questions. We have additional books on each subject should more study be advisable or necessary for you. Finally, the more you study, the better prepared you will be. This book is intended to be the last thing you study before you walk into the examination room. Prior study of relevant texts is also recommended. NLC publishes some of these in our Fundamental Series. Knowledge and good sense are important factors in passing your exam. Good luck also helps. So now study this Passbook, absorb the material contained within and take that knowledge into the examination. Then do your best to pass that exam.

EXAMINATION SECTION

EXAMINATION SECTION
TEST 1

OFFICIAL DICTATION

(175 Words per minute for five (5) minutes)

      This Court has granted a writ of certiorari to review a final order of the New York Court of Appeals, which affirmed an order of the Appellate Division of the Supreme Court of the State of New York, First Judicial Department. That order disapproved petitioner's claim that certain sales taxes were due and owing to it by the respondent. The sum in dispute is two thousand, nine hundred and eighty-three dollars, with interest, and the period involved covers the years nineteen seventy-one and nineteen seventy-two.

      The sole ground for the rejection of the petitioner's claim by the order under review was that the sales tax law as here applied violated the commerce clause of the federal constitution. The respondent in this proceeding is the Smith Office Machine Company, an Illinois firm engaged in the manufacture and sale of office machines to buyers in all parts of the country. With the Green Adding Machine Company, its wholly owned subsidiary and agent, it maintains offices, workrooms and a stockroom in New York City. There it sells, rents, repairs and services office machines and parts of office machines. Its New York City staff consists of a sales manager and several sales representatives. Only those New York City sales which are filled for the New York Office by shipment from the Illinois factory are the subject of this suit.

      The respondent's products are office machines in standard sizes and models, not designed or altered to fill any special orders. The company does not accept any special orders for office machines. A large supply of office machines, with a market value of at least eighty-five thousand dollars, is always kept on hand in its New York City stockrooms. However, the company does not fill its local orders from local stock, but employs an interstate procedure. Orders are taken by the company's New York office and forwarded to the Chicago office. Every order states the model number, style, size and price of each machine sold. The order does not name the place of shipment of the machines, nor is there any evidence that the purchaser knows the place from which the machines are to be shipped to his office. Since the respondent bears the shipping costs and risk of loss, the customer actually purchases the machines in delivered condition.

      All orders taken are subject to confirmation by the Chicago office. However, the procedure as to confirmation appears to be largely routine. Prices are fixed by the sales office in New York City on the basis of a standard price list. The trade-in value of old machines is fixed by the sales manager in New York City. There is no evidence that the Chicago office ever fails to confirm, nor is there any evidence that the customer is ever notified of confirmation. As a matter of fact, the order form contains no space for confirmation. The requirement of Chicago confirmation appears to serve no purpose other than to ascertain errors in price quoting and to allow for credit checking.

      The respondent packs the machine in a carton and ships it, not to the customer, but to its New York City office. The customer is not concerned at all with this shipment, is not the consignee, is not protected by the insurance, and, consequently, does not pay the freight charges. The respondent must ship the office machine to its New York workroom because the machine on its arrival there is frequently not in a deliverable condition. There is a great deal of breakage in transit which must be repaired in the New York workroom. Even where there has been no breakage, testing and adjusting must be done there. These tasks of testing and adjusting often take three or four days, and it is not until they are finished that the local office can make delivery to the customer.

The contractual obligations of the respondent do not cease with delivery. Each contract of sale requires the company to keep the office machine in good repair for one year from the date of delivery, without charge to the customer. To fulfill this obligation, the respondent renders a free monthly maintenance service of inspection, oiling, and cleaning. When repairs of a substantial nature are needed, the work is done in New York City. While the machine is at the workroom for repair, a loan is made of another machine from the company's stock.

The recital of all these facts serves to show clearly that the tax in question does not interfere with the power reserved to the federal government to regulate interstate commerce. This court has never invalidated a state statute unless it has found that the statute, as a matter of fact, subjected interstate commerce to a greater burden, or to the danger of a greater burden, than would arise if the commerce were not being done. This court has very recently sustained a tax identical with the tax in question in every factual respect in a case involving the same petititioner and this same method of selling and shipping goods across state lines. Therefore, we believe that factual analysis reveals that this tax does not impose a burden upon interstate commerce. The final order and judgment should be reversed.

TEST 2

OFFICIAL DICTATION

(175 Words per minute for five(5) minutes)

The Supreme Court granted the motions made by the plaintiff, George Jones, to strike out the answer, to dismiss the counterclaim and to grant summary judgment. The court then appointed a referee to compute the amount due and owing to the plaintiff. The referee received and considered all the pleadings, including the answer and the bill of particulars submitted by the defendant, Albert Smith, as well as certain receipts. These receipts showed that the defendant had paid a total of ten thousand, nine hundred and eight dollars and forty-nine cents for interest and for amortization of the principal amount of the mortgages as well as for taxes and for the cost of defending an earlier action to foreclose the first mortgage on the property. The referee reported that the total balance due to the plaintiff was eighteen thousand, four hundred and twenty-seven dollars and eighty-five cents. The court granted a judgment for that amount, together with costs and other allowances, and ordered foreclosure and sale of property.

After this judgment had $\underset{X}{1}$ been granted, the defendant moved for an order to direct a rehearing of his motion to dismiss the complaint and for leave to submit an amended answer. The proposed amended answer, as attached to the moving papers, contained defenses similar to those interposed in the original answer. One new defense, alleging forgiveness by the plaintiff of part of the principal sum due, was offered but rejected by the court because of lack of evidence. In this defense, the defendant, Albert Smith, claimed that a total of three thousand, two hundred and twenty-six dollars had been forgiven by the plaintiff during the period from August, nineteen sixty-six until March, nineteen sixty-eight.

From these orders and the final judgment, the defendant has appealed to this court. During pendency of this appeal, the defendant assigned his entire interest in the property to the White Star Corporation. The date of this assignment was March twelfth, nineteen sixty-nine. Shortly thereafter, Smith attempted to withdraw his answer in the foreclosure action. He also agreed to the entry $\underset{X}{2}$ of a final judgment and, at the same time, stipulated that he would withdraw his appeal to this court. The motives prompting Albert Smith to this unusual course of conduct are not as yet apparent. The White Star Corporation charges that Smith's action was prompted by the desire to deprive it of its rightful interest in the property and that all these steps were taken in collusion with the plaintiff.

After the corporation had received the assignment of the property, it promptly applied in Special Term of the Supreme Court to be substituted as a party defendant in place of the defendant, Albert Smith. Special Term did not pass upon the merits of the application but denied the motion solely on the grounds that the issues involved were already on appeal before this court; The corporation thereupon made a motion to be substituted in place of Albert Smith before this court on the argument of this appeal. This court has examined the assignment to the corporation and finds said assignment to be legal and binding, $\underset{X}{3}$ Under that assignment, the corporation is sub-rogated to all the rights held by Albert Smith. This court further rules that Albert Smith had no right to take further action in the litigation after assigning his interest in the property to the White Star Corporation. His attempt to withdraw his answer, to consent to entry of judgment and to abandon his appeal are all Ineffectual. The White Star Corporation is entitled to be substituted as a party in interest in place of Albert Smith and its motion for such relief is therefore granted. All papers hereafter submitted should indicate that the corporation is the true party whose present interest is adverse to that of the plaintiff, George Jones.

This court is now prepared to consider the merits of the appeal. The present defendant argues that triable issues are involved and that summary judgment in favor of the plaintiff should not have been granted. In his answer in Supreme Court, the original defendant pleaded the defense of the Statute of Limitations. The court properly disposed of that

[4] defense by reference to the mortgage moratorium statute. That statute prohibits the bringing of foreclosure suit where the debor had defaulted in reducing only the principal of the debt. In the case at bar, the defendant Albert Smith was not in arrears in payment of interest on the mortgage debt but only in reduction of the face amount of the debt.

The substantive issues of the case are therefore open for our consideration. Albert Smith never contended that the bond and mortgage were not legal and binding instruments when made. His main defense to the action was that the principal sum due had been reduced to less than one-third of the original amount, partly by payment and partly by forgiveness of certain installments. The Supreme Court rejected both of these defenses on the grounds that the defendant had failed to produce any substantial evidence in favor of his contentions. However, as the present appellant contends that credible evidence as to certain payments does exist, we direct that a trial of those issues be held. [5]

EXAMINATION SECTION
TEST 1

OFFICIAL DICTATION
1st CASE
(175 Words Per Minute For Five (5) Minutes)

The Fulton Savings Bank was the owner of two separate mortgages, each in the principal sum of fourteen thousand five hundred dollars, which were liens on two separate premises near the intersection of Broadway and 42nd Street in the Borough of Manhattan. The principal sums were due on these mortgages on January tenth, nineteen eighty-eight. The record indicates that six years later, Edward Thomas, the mortgagor, was in default for taxes, water, and interest in the amount of fourteen hundred ninety-eight dollars and fifty cents.

The principal sum of fourteen thousand five hundred dollars due on each of these mortgages, according to their terms, on January tenth, nineteen eighty-eight, was also unpaid.

In order to insure preservation of the property, Edward Thomas, the owner of the premises, executed and delivered an assignment of rents in which an agent was appointed to manage the premises and apply the rents and profits of said premises for disbursements for the ordinary and proper maintenance and upkeep of the mortgaged premises. The instrument also irrevocably $\overset{1}{x}$ assigned to the mortgagee, the Fulton Savings Bank, all sums received by the owner from the aforementioned agent to be applied in its direction and in any order it might determine, on account of the arrears of taxes, water rates, assessments, fire insurance premiums, premiums on liability policies, interest, and installments of principal. It further provided that the aforesaid agency should continue and the powers of the said agent should remain in full force and effect until all arrears of taxes and other charges, which might be liens upon said mortgaged premises in priority to the above-mentioned mortgage, and all arrears of principal and interest upon said mortgage debt had been fully paid.

This arrangement still continues in force and effect, never having been rescinded or modified, and as of the present date, the record indicates that the principal of each mortgage has been reduced to ten thousand eight hundred dollars with interest of six percent from said date. All other obligations are paid.

Recently, John Alexander, owner of mortgages on these premises, $\overset{2}{x}$ junior in priority to the mortgages above referred to, commenced an action to foreclose his mortgages, and in that action a receiver of the rents was duly appointed by an ex parte order of this court. The receiver immediately investigated the situation. Said receiver, informed of the foregoing assignment, has now moved this court for an order restraining the Fulton Savings Bank and its agents from interfering with him in the collection of the rents, and directing said bank and its agents to turn over to him any of the rents they may have collected from time of his appointment as receiver herein.

By a separate motion, the Fulton Savings Bank and its agent have moved to vacate the order appointing the receiver in the action to foreclose the junior mortgages. The bank contends that by virtue of the assignment above described, it is entitled to apply the net rentals accruing from the premises on account of the principal as well as the interest secured by its aforesaid mortgages until the same shall have $\overset{3}{x}$ been paid.

    The attorney representing the plaintiff in the motion to foreclose the junior mortgages has submitted an affidavit in support of the receiver's motion and in opposition to that made by the Bank. He contends that a reading of the assignment in question indicates the intention of the parties to terminate the assignment when all of the arrears which existed at the time the assignment was executed have been paid and not, as contended by the Bank, when the principals of the mortgages have been fully paid. Plaintiff further contends that the net income from premises is in excess of the three percent statutory amortization to which the first mortgagee is entitled under the present moratory statutes, that said first mortgagee is not entitled to be paid any additional sums on account of principal beyond three percent, and that to hold otherwise would unjustly deprive the second mortgagee of his legal rights under the junior mortgages covering the premises in question.

    Whatever view one might take of the first contention set forth $\overset{4}{x}$ in the preceding paragraph as urged by the attorney for the junior mortgagee, the result of the present applications must be the same. When the foregoing assignments of rents were executed, the so-called *moratory statutes* were in force. Under the provisions of Section ten seventy-seven a of the Civil Practice Act, effective August twenty-sixth, nineteen fifty-three, the right to foreclose a mortgage by reason of the non-payment of past due water taxes, other taxes, and interest was not disturbed.

    Prior to the enactment of the moratory statutes, a different rule would have applied. Indeed, had the assignment of rents in this case been executed prior to the enactment of the moratory statutes, the bank's rights thereunder could not thereafter have been disturbed as they were vested property and contract rights. In this case, however, the assignment was executed and delivered on March twenty-seventh, nineteen fifty-four, after the moratory statute, Section ten seventy-seven, a and c of the Civil Practice Act, became effective. Thus the statute does apply. $\overset{5}{x}$

OFFICIAL DICTATION
2nd CASE
(175 Words Per Minute For Five (5) Minutes)

The record before us indicates that the Lehigh Valley National Bank and Trust Company deeded to the Lakeside Corporation, a parcel of land, used as a children's camp, on Silver Lake in Essex County. The deed was recorded September 24, 1987, Upon the execution and delivery of the deed, the Lakeside Corporation gave the bank a first mortgage on the property in the total sum of twenty-one thousand dollars. This mortgage was actually recorded in the Essex County Clerk's office shortly after its delivery.

A few weeks thereafter the Lakeside Corporation gave a second mortgage on the same premises to the plaintiff and to the defendant Jones to secure the payment of the sum of eighty-five hundred dollars. The plaintiff and the defendant Jones each owned a one-half interest in the second mortgage. This mortgage was not acknowledged or recorded until nearly five years had elapsed. It covered not only the real estate but all the fixtures, articles of personal property, equipment, and other furnishings in the buildings on $\underset{X}{^1}$ the premises, or then or thereafter attached to or used in connection with the premises. It also provided that should the lien of the mortgage be held inferior to the lien of a conditional sale contract or chattel mortgage covering any of the personal property, then, in the event of default, all interest of the mortgagor in such personal property was assigned to the mortgagee together with the credit for any payments made thereon by the mortgagor.

By deed dated June fifteenth, nineteen ninety-two, and recorded six or seven months later, the Lakeside Corporation conveyed the premises to Frank Albert, a relative of defendant Jones. Two judgments were secured against the Lakeside Corporation. One judgment in favor of the State Industrial Commission for fourteen hundred twenty-eight dollars and thirty-three cents was docketed within a few days and another in favor of Mason and Company for seven hundred and thirteen dollars and eighty cents was docketed on September third, nineteen ninety-two.

Shortly thereafter, as the record indicates, Frank Albert leased the property $\underset{X}{^2}$ to defendant George J. Robinson for a term expiring on September thirtieth, nineteen ninety-seven. The lease included use of the real property, buildings, and equipment then on the premises, or stored elsewhere, except for certain specified articles. In addition to the annual rent payable under the lease, there was an agreement by Robinson to employ Frank Jones, husband of defendant, Ethel Jones, as camp superintendent and purchasing agent, at a specified salary. There was also a provision for the payment of a certain amount for various expenses which included interest on the mortgages, insurance, and taxes. The lease also provided that an inventory of equipment owned by the lessor and the lessee should be taken and that such equipment should remain their personal property. All buildings and other structures erected upon the premises became the property of the lessor but the cost of all equipment purchased was to be adjusted between the parties.

The record further indicates that plaintiff instituted an action to foreclose the second mortgage. A supplemental summons and an amended complaint $\underset{X}{^3}$ in that action were served on defendant Robinson on August twenty-fifth, nineteen ninety-two. Jones, one of the owners of the mortgage, refused to become a plaintiff and was made a defendant in that action. Defendant Robinson appeared in the action and served an answer to the amended complaint in which he denied on information and belief the material allegations thereof. In addition to that, he alleged six separate and distinct defenses.

The first defense pleaded the six-year statute of limitations.

As the second defense, Robinson alleged that the lease had been given to him by defendant Jones, by authority of and for the benefit of plaintiff. He further alleged that under the terms of the lease, plaintiff and defendant Jones had covenanted that Robinson should quietly enjoy the premises and hence that the plaintiff was estopped from asserting any claim against Robinson.

The third defense alleged Robinson had placed certain buildings, fixtures, and chattels on the premises, for use in the operation of the camp, which were not covered by the mortgages[4] and that these structures could be removed without substantial injury to the freehold.

As the fourth defense, Robinson alleged that plaintiff had ratified the lease and thereby acknowledged the right of Robinson to remove the property.

The fifth defense stated that the mortgage was void for want of consideration.

For a sixth defense and counterclaim against the plaintiff and defendant Jones, Robinson alleged that Jones and Albert had agreed in the lease to pay off the mortgage and that foreclosure thereof would damage him in the sum of twenty-five thousand dollars. Robinson demanded that the complaint be dismissed and that he have judgment against the defendants Jones and Albert for the damages that he would sustain.

Defendants Jones and Albert served replies denying the material allegations of the defenses and the counterclaim and asked for judgment dismissing them. Plaintiff moved to strike out the first, fourth, and fifth defenses contained in the answer on the ground that the defenses were insufficient in law. By these motions plaintiff is attempting to obtain decision before trial.[5]

TEST 2

OFFICIAL DICTATION
OPENING
(175 Words Per Minute - 3 Minutes)

Mr. Cohen's question is rather broad. If he intended to inquire solely as to the effect of failure to give notice under the circumstances stated, the answer, I think, is simple. The principle is well established that the provisions of section 44 of the Personal Property Law must be strictly construed (Mott v. Reeves, 125 Misc., 511, aff'd 213 App. Div., 718, aff'd 246 N.Y., 567). The section is barren of any requirement, or even a suggestion of requirement, that the purchaser make an independent search for creditors. The Bulk Sales Law requires that those creditors must be notified whose names and addresses are stated in the list furnished by the seller or of whom the purchaser has knowledge. That does not mean possible creditors, but known creditors. There is no basis for reading into the statute that which is not explicitly stated therein, nor which may not be $\overset{1}{x}$ fairly implied therefrom. It seems clear that under the circumstances stated by Mr. Cohen the purchaser may proceed with complete assurance against liability to creditors if any later appear. Must the purchaser, however, against the possibility of undisclosed creditors, make and keep the inventory called for? Caution requires an affirriative reply in the absence of adjudication on this point.

Many lawyers have deemed it sufficient to take the affidavit of the seller and to withhold from the purchase price a sum sufficient to pay the creditors disclosed to the purchaser, without complying with the other provisions of the statute relating to inventory and notice. Under such circumstances, would not a creditor, undisclosed and unknown to the purchaser, properly seek to impose liability on the purchaser because each requirement of the statute had not been complied with? The question does not appear to have been presented to the courts.

Another troublesome $\overset{2}{x}$ point concerns the making of the inventory by the seller. What is reasonable diligence in ascertaining the cost price to the seller of each article included in the sale (and there may be thousands of similar articles purchased at various tines, the original cost of which can be traced, if at all, only with the greatest difficulty), and how the purchaser (who must pay the penalty) can effectively control the diligence of the seller is perplexing indeed to the lawyer who must advise the purchaser in the transaction.

Annoying, too, is the requirement that the notice to creditors must be *of the proposed sale and of the price, terms, and conditions thereof.* There may be a lengthy contract, with multitudinous terms, each of which is an integral part of the contract, but in most of which the creditor can have no legitimate interest. Nevertheless a precise compliance with the terms x of the statute would require the placing of the entire contract in the hands of every creditor, large or small.

EXAMINATION SECTION
TESTIMONY

OFFICIAL DICTATION
PART I

(175 Words per minute for three (3) minutes)

We address ourselves at the outset to the question of whether or not there was an investment of the funds of the aforementioned estate in the mortgages in question. The trial court held that there was an investment, whereas the Appellate Division held that there was not. In our statement of the facts we have outlined the details with reference to the disposition of the funds of the said estate after the moneys were deposited with the City Officer, with particular reference to that portion of the moneys belonging to a certain firm of attorneys. The City Officer's records and the testimony of one witness show clearly that the funds deposited in the said estate were actually used to pay off moneys due to certain accounts and that the shares in two mortgages, formerly allocated to these accounts, were allocated on the books of the City Officer to the said $\frac{1}{x}$ estate.

This transaction, in our view, amounted to investments of the funds of the said estate in the two mortgages and the trial court so found. The defendants urge, however, that the allocations made by the City Officer were mere bookkeeping entries and not, therefore, investments of the estate funds. However, the practice followed with reference to the said estate was typical of that employed with respect to many other accounts and has frequently been held to constitute an investment. One court said that the money was paid to the City Officer and was immediately deposited by him to the credit of his account in a designated bank. It apparently remained there on deposit for a few days when it was invested in a manner evidently common in his office, but which is not criticized by the parties interested in the fund.

The City Officer held a mortgage which covered $\frac{2}{x}$ certain vacant lots in the City of New York. He was later ordered to pay over certain moneys to the persons entitled, and desiring to keep this mortgage and certain others in which those moneys had been invested, he used the moneys deposited, in this case, to make the payments required. The balance of the fund was thereupon deposited in the trust company where it remained until the following year, when it was invested in a similar manner, and by the same process, in certain other mortgages held by the City Officer.

Another Court in a similar case referred to this practice of the City Officer, several times in the course of its opinion and always spoke of the transaction as an investment. It had been customary for the City Officer to make payment in cash of amounts which had been invested by transferring the investment to any desired fund. $\frac{3}{x}$

PART II
(Testimony of 175 words per minute for 5 minutes by 4 voices)

P.Q.   Now, suppose we clear up the matter about what attention you received after your accident. You say you were first picked up on a stretcher and taken to the nearest hospital emergency ward. Is that right, and was anything done for you there?

W.A.   I think I was kept there about an hour while they were calling up an ambulance. They didn't try to do anything for me there, although my hip was paining me badly. I believe they didn't have any accommodations at that hospital for people with injured legs. It was a mistake to take me there in the first place.

P.Q.   In other words, you were there about an hour and nothing was done for you. You were just lying out on the stretcher for all that time, and you said your left hip kept paining you ---

D.   I object to this line of questioning. Let him ask one thing at a time.

J.   They are simple questions as to what the situation was. Continue.

P.Q.   Your left hip kept paining you, and later on they had $\underset{x}{\overset{1}{\rule{0.6em}{0.4pt}}}$ occasion to bring the ambulance, is that right?

W.A.   Yes, it was paining me, of course, and after the ambulance came they took me down town to the hospital and put me into the emergency ward, and they called up my doctor.

P.Q.   That was about two and a half hours after the accident occurred, and while you were in the emergency ward, was anything done for you while you were waiting for your doctor to arrive?

W.A.   Well, I was in agony all the time, but nothing happened till my doctor came and he had me put on a bed, and he rigged the bed up in such a way that a pulley could be put on to keep my leg stretched.

P.A.   How long did you remain in bed with this pulley contraption attached to your leg, and what other things were done for you?

W.A.   Oh, I was in bed for three or for days with the pulley on, and they took x-ray pictures with the machine right there while I was in bed, and nest thing, $\underset{x}{\overset{2}{\rule{0.6em}{0.4pt}}}$ they took me into the operating room and gave me ether. I was under that ether for three or four hours, and when I woke up, they had a cast from my toes to my armpit.

P.Q.   Before you went under the ether and during the five or six days that you were lying with this pulley on your left foot, did the left leg or the left hip hurt you?

W.A. Oh, yes, it hurt me all the time both before and after the cast was put on and I was so bad that they gave me needles. They gave me needles for about four weeks, till the doctor said they could not give me any more and that I would have to do without it. I never slept a wink from when I went in there until I got out, except in the day time, I might doze off for a few minutes, that is all. And I asked the doctor couldn't he do anything for me---

J. I think we should not have any conversations. $\frac{3}{x}$ He must not tell us what the doctor said to him. Just let him tell how he felt himself.

D. Yes, and I object to this line of testimony as purely speculative and further, on the ground that it is not on the proper basis. Let the witness be told to answer directly. The rest is incompetent, irrelevant and immaterial.

J. Let him proceed.

P.Q. How long was this plaster cast on you and how did you feel? Were you lying on your back? When did they finally take it off?

W.A. The plaster cast was on me about ten weeks, and by that time I was all in, my back cut, and I was sore all over. I lost about 40 pounds and I was perspiring all the time I was in the cast. Then they cut off the top part of the cast and let a little air in, but I had to lie on my back on the other., half for another two or three weeks. It must have been over three months before they measured $\frac{4}{x}$ me for a brace and gave me crutches.
The first day I got up, I could only sit up for an hour, but every day they put me in a wheel chair for a little longer and at last I took a change with the crutches and the brace, and I could just navigate.

P.Q. You had some expenses while in the hospital, didn't you? And did you pay these bills week by week as they became due?

W.A. Yes, and I have all receipts here. ---

J. What is the total amount? Instead of offering all the separate receipts in evidence, just add them up and tell us the amount.

D. We will concede the amount is a fair and reasonable charge.

J. Why don't you say what the amount is and they will concede it. Let your assistant add up the amount and they will concede, that is what he had paid.

P.Q. Now, you had bills for the doctor, for braces and crutches and even for the ambulance. Didn't you?

4 (#1)

W.A.   Yes, I paid about a thousand dollars. $\frac{5}{x}$

PART III
(Testimony for 4 minutes by four voices)

P.Q.   Now, doctor, you may refresh your recollection from this record as far as-you can. Did you see the plaintiff soon after he came to the hospital, and will you describe his condition at the time you saw him to the Court and Jury? ---

        J.   Doctor, you can look at that record to refresh your recollection, but the hospital record is what they call hearsay evidence. It might be made up by anybody. The best evidence is the testimony of you yourself, but if you should forget anything, you may look through that to refresh your memory, but do not read from it.

W.A.   I saw him the day he was admitted, and he was complaining of pain in the region of his left hip. The left leg was pulled out from the body, the left foot turned out from the body, and he was unable to lift the left leg from the bed. There was pain when we tried to move the leg in the region of the left hip and abnormal mobility which made me think that he had a fracture.

P.Q.   If you recall, what did you do for him at that time and later on, when you took charge $\frac{1}{x}$ of developments?

W.A,   We had x-rays taken shortly after his admission and then he was put in a form of traction with pulleys and weights extending to his leg to try and pull it down into position. At the end of two or three days the leg was pulled down sufficiently and then I took him to the operating room and under an anaesthetic, I applied the plaster of Paris cast.

P.Q.   How many x-ray pictures did you have taken altogether, and what facts did they show?

W.A,   Ten pictures altogether. They showed the fracture, and from time to time, the progress of the healing, and they indicated what were the next steps to be taken. On the basis of these x-rays, we know how to apply the cast, we can see how the fracture is healing, the new bone forming, and then we can judge when it is time to remove part or all of the cast.

P.Q.   Will you describe generally his condition at the time he left the hospital, and what you believe to be his present condition.

W.A.   Well, he left the hospital wearing a splint which did not allow any weight bearing on the left leg itself, but allowed him to $\frac{2}{x}$ walk. After wearing this for three months we commenced to let him bear weight on his leg. When I examined him last week his left leg appeared to be about an inch shorter than his right leg. It can move fairly easily in and out, though the muscles in that leg differ in size from those in the right leg. The condition is permanent, I would say.

P.Q. Supposing, doctor, that a man of fifty-four years of age was walking along a sidewalk on which snow and ice has been packed down---

  J. I think we could save the time of the Court and Jury by stating, without putting any hypothetical question, that such a fall could precipitate the injuries described by the doctor.

  D. I will join that concession, except that I would like the doctor to state that he considered that a good union or repair resulted, if that is so.

W.A. Well, callous had formed and nature had produced a good union, although the fractured portion was a little thicker than the other side. For a man of his age I think he got a very good result, but of course there was some shortening and loss of flexibility. $\frac{3}{x}$

PART IV
(Charge of 175 words per minute for 5 minutes by the Judge)

 Ladies and gentlemen of the jury, this action is brought by the plaintiff to recover damages for personal injuries which he alleges he sustained by reason of the negligence of these defendants. The plaintiff maintains that while he was walking on the southerly sidewalk, before referred to, he slipped and fell to the ground as a result of which he sustained the injuries which you have heard descibed. The plaintiff contends that the City of New York negligently permitted snow and ice to accumulate and remain upon the sidewalk, rendering passage on the sidewalk dangerous to persons walking upon it.

 The plaintiff further contends that the defendant was also careless and negligent in that during the course of his business he permitted water to be discharged from his premises, flow upon the sidewalk in winter weather and freeze, thus creating a dangerous and unsafe condition. The plaintiff further claims that the condition of the sidewalk such as you have heard described existed for some

time prior to the accident and that the defendants had notice $\frac{1}{x}$ of the defective condition and should have remedied it. The defendants deny any and all responsibility for the accident. They contend that the sidewalk under the existing conditions and circumstances was maintained in a safe manner, and that the accident was caused not by any omission on their part but by the carelessness of the plaintiff himself. The defendant denies that he permitted water to be discharged from his premises and freeze upon the sidewalk and insists that he took all the proper precautions that might reasonably be expected of him in the maintenance of his premises. Both he and the City contend that at the time of the accident and prior thereto the winter weather was such that they did all that was humanly possible and that, therefore, they were in no manner careless or negligent.

Now, except as I have stated here, I feel I cannot aid you by a discussion of the evidence. The testimony of the several witnesses is fresh in your minds and your recollection is as good, if not $\frac{2}{x}$ better than mine. The case has been tried by experienced and able counsel on both sides and if I should pick out portions of the testimony for discussion I might unconsciously lead you to suppose that I considered important matters which you considered unimportant and vice versa. So as to the facts, *I* am going to leave the case entirely with you, leaving it to you to discuss the testimony wholly uninfluenced by anything that *I* say to you concerning it.

Now, this is a negligence action. Negligence may be defined as the failure or the omission to do some act or perform some duty which one person owes to another. More simply defined, it is the absence of such care as a reasonably prudent person would be expected to use under the circumstances. Before the plaintiff can recover, the law places on him the burden of proving to your satisfaction by a fair preponderance of the credible evidence that he was injured by reason of the negligence of these defendants. He must prove that $\frac{3}{x}$ the accident was caused solely and wholly by the negligence of the defendants or either of them, and if he fails in that, then no matter how much you may sympathize with the misfortune that has overtaken him, he may not in justice recover damages and your verdict must be for the defendants.

The plaintiff must also prove that this accident in which it is claimed he was injured was not brought about or contributed to by any negligence, however slight on his part, for if you find that the plaintiff was guilty of contributory negligence, even in the slightest degree, he cannot recover against these defendants. The fact that an accident happened and that the plaintiff was injured are not in themselves reasons sufficient for you to determine that the plaintiff must recover, for there is no presumption of negligence to be drawn from the mere happening of an accident. A further burden resting upon the plaintiff is to prove that the accident in which it is claimed that he was injured was a $\frac{4}{x}$ competent producing cause of the injuries claimed to have been sustained and for the condition it is claimed the plaintiff is now suffering from.

I charge you, ladies and gentlemen, that the defendants are not insurers of the safety of pedestrians. The City of New York is not expected to maintain its streets and roads, in such an absolutely perfect condition as to render accidents impossible. It is expected to use reasonable care and prudence in detecting and remedying any defect which might be anticipated as dangerous and liable to cause an accident. The measure of its duty in this respect is reasonable care.

Actual notice means what it says. By constructive notice is meant that a condition has existed for a sufficient length of time as to charge one with presumptive knowledge of that condition. It is for you to say whether the time that this condition existed, if at all, was sufficiently long enough to charge the City with constructive notice.

Now, I thank you all for your attention. Are there any questions? $\frac{5}{x}$

EXAMINATION SECTION
TESTIMONY

(175 Words per minute - 5 minutes)

Cross examination by defendant's counsel:

QUESTION: Do you remember the month that the man from the City saw you in this case?

ANSWER: I remember it very well.

QUESTION: What month was that?

ANSWER: That was the day before Thanksgiving.

QUESTION: He wrote down what you told him, at that time, did he not?

ANSWER: I do not know what he did.

QUESTION: You were there. Did you not see him?

ANSWER: I was there. Sure I saw him.

QUESTION: I ask you this question: What he wrote down was what you told him?

    Plaintiff's Counsel: I object. The witness is not competent to testify to that.
    The Court: No, unless he read it.

QUESTION: Did he not write down what you told him?

ANSWER: I do not know what he did.

QUESTION: Did he not read something to you?

ANSWER: No. He was propounding questions to me.

QUESTION: Do you say that he did not read you, the statement he made?

ANSWER: No, I did not give him any. And the doctors did not give him any. He wanted them both to give him statements.

QUESTION: Did the man tell you from what department of the City of New York he was?

ANSWER: Yes.

QUESTION: What department?

ANSWER: The Corporation Counsel's office.

QUESTION: Or was it the Department of Finance, or the Comptroller's office?

ANSWER: No, he said he was from the Corporation Counsel's office.

QUESTION: What was his name? Do you remember his name?

ANSWER: No. He did not introduce himself.

QUESTION: Do you remember telling the man from the City that you did not know the number of the house in front of which Doctor MacDonald fell?

ANSWER: I know, if I told him anything, it was ---

QUESTION: You did not tell him anything?

ANSWER: No, and there is no witness to corroborate it. He wanted me to sign a paper, and he wanted the doctors to sign a paper. He was the means of having me fired out of the hospital, 1 was there through courtesy, not because I was mentally disabled.

    Defendant's Counsel: Will you please keep still? I ask that all the answer be striken out.

    The Court: Strike it out.

QUESTION: Did he want you to sign a paper?

ANSWER: Yes.

QUESTION: These are the papers he wanted you to sign; is that correct?

ANSWER: I do $\overset{2}{\underset{X}{}}$ not know. I did not look at them. I did not rise. He sat in a chair. I was sitting farther than the table away from him.

QUESTION: Did you sign anything?

    Plaintiff's counsel: He stated he did not see it.

ANSWER: I never signed anything.

QUESTION: And, after you told this man from the Corporation Counsel's office or from the City of New York this story, he wrote it down and read the statement to you?

ANSWER: He did not get any story from me. He asked Doctor Schatz if he would be a witness to the fact. I told him I would sign nothing. And Doctor Schatz told him he would sign nothing either.

QUESTION: I am not asking you anything that Doctor Schatz told. I am talking about you, only.

ANSWER: That is what happened there. I did not want to be botheredwith it.

QUESTION: Did he not read this all over to you, and did you not say that it was correct in all respects?

ANSWER: No, I never gave the man a statement.

    Defendant's Counsel: That is all.

    Plaintiff's Counsel: May I have $\overset{3}{\underset{X}{}}$ the privilege of a few questions, your Honor?

    The Court: Proceed.

Re-direct Examination by Plaintiff's Counsel:

QUESTION: I hand you Plaintiff's Exhibit 5 and ask you to look at it carefully, also Defendant's Exhibit B. Do you observe, from these two exhibits, that there are five sections of the ventilation grating?

3 (#1)

ANSWER: Yes.

QUESTION: In front of 711 and 715 Replogle Avenue?

ANSWER: Yes.

QUESTION: And the five sections are both shown in these two exhibits, are they?

ANSWER: Yes.

QUESTION: Do you observe also, that each of those five sections is again subdivided into four parts?

ANSWER: Yes, sir.

QUESTION: Four parts in.width?

ANSWER: Yes, sir.

QUESTION: Now, when you testified on cross examination that, so far as you remember, the pegs were only in front of the section where the Reverend Mackler fell ---

ANSWER: Yes.

QUESTION: Did you or did you not mean, or tell me what you meant. Did you mean that the pegs were entirely across the four subdivisions of the southern section?

ANSWER: Yes.

> Defendant's Counsel: Now, wait, please. If your Honor please, I object to this, on the ground that I asked the question and your Honor asked the question, and $\underset{X}{\overset{4}{-}}$ I asked the witness if he understood your Honor's question.
> The Court: Yes, but he answered both ways across. I am going to let him straighten it out.

QUESTION: In referring to this grating here, let us be sure we understand our terminology. I am going to call these five different parts five sections, and each of these five sections in turn has four parts.

ANSWER: Yes.

QUESTION: Now, counsel, up to this time, called each of those four p.arts sections; but let us forget that terminology a minute. Were there pegs all the way across the southern end of the southern section, which included four parts?

ANSWER: I believe they were.

Re-cross Examination by Defendant's Counsel:

QUESTION: I asked you -- pointed out on this photograph that I held in front of the jury--- I have this up, and I asked you whether the pegs ran across from one side to the other, and you said no, did you not?

ANSWER: Well, because I looked through two pairs of glasses, and it looked the same.

QUESTION: You saw the picture up there, and I asked you to look at $\underset{X}{5}$ it.

4 (#1)

Direct Examination by Plaintiff's Counsel:

QUESTION: Do you know the plaintiff in this case?

ANSWER: I do.

QUESTION: Did you see the plaintiff in this case on December 22?

ANSWER: I did.

QUESTION: Will you tell the Court and jury under what circumstances you saw him and describe for the court and jury also what you saw about him?

ANSWER: Well, the doorbell rang. I went upstairs and answered it. A gentleman stood there with a bloody handkerchief to his mouth, and he asked whether he could see the doctor. He was very much shaken and agitated, and, in fact, he was trembling. And I said I was afraid he could not see the doctor, because he was ill.

  Defendant's Counsel: I beg your pardon. I am sorry to interrupt, but we cannot have anything like that.
  The Court: You cannot have any conversation. How was the doctor? Was he ill?

QUESTION: Just describe what you saw yourself about the Reverend MacDonald.

ANSWER: He stood there with his handkerchief to his face. His handkerchief was bloody, and he was pale. In fact, he was livid.

  Plaintiff's Counsel: A little louder. I cannot hear you.
  The Witness: He was livid.

QUESTION: By that do you mean his face was white?

ANSWER: No. Livid is something more than white. Livid is a sort of blue white. It is worse than pale, if you ever saw it.

QUESTION: What else did you notice about Doctor Mackler?

ANSWER: Well, I noticed that he was trembling. In fact, he was shaking so much that I was---well, just a little bit nervous.

QUESTION: Was the doctor ill that day?

ANSWER: Yes, he was; but he was not in bed.

  Plaintiff's Counsel: That is all.

Cross Examination by Defendant's Counsel:

QUESTION: Mr. Gorman, was the doctor out on Sunday, last Sunday? ANSWER: Last Sunday, I do not know. He was out one day to get a newspaper; but I do not know whether it was Saturday or Sunday.

QUESTION: Was he out on Sunday?

ANSWER: Let's see. I cannot answer that. I do not know whether he was or not. I was not home most of the day.

5 (#1)

The Court: Next question.

QUESTION: Do you know whether any subpoena has been served on the doctor personally to come to court?

ANSWER: Not to my knowledge.

> Defendant's Counsel: That is all.
> Plaintiff's Counsel: May I ask one other question, your Honor?
> The Court: Yes.

Re-direct Examination by Plaintiff's Counsel:

QUESTION: Did you recognize Doctor Mackler when you first saw him that day?

ANSWER: No, I did not.

QUESTION: You say he had the handkerchief over his mouth this way?

ANSWER: Yes.

QUESTION: How long had you known him, Mr. Gorman?

ANSWER: That is a little hard to answer; but I should say over a period of—well, I could not answer that--I could answer it, perhaps, in another way.

QUESTION: Can you tell us about how long a time? That is all.

ANSWER: I am not very much---possibly, over a period of ten years.

QUESTION: You say that, when he came over there, his handkerchief was over his mouth that way?

ANSWER: Yes.

QUESTION: You did not recognize him?

ANSWER: I did not recognize him.

Re-cross Examination by Defendant's Counsel:

QUESTION: Was there not anything about his dress that indicated that it was Doctor Mackler?

ANSWER: Why, yes, he had his regular clerical garb on, as far as I can remember.

QUESTION: How long was he talking to you, Mr Gorman?

ANSWER: Not very long.

QUESTION: Would you say ten minutes?

ANSWER: No, not as long as that.

QUESTION: Five minutes?

ANSWER: Oh, yes, I think so.

QUESTION: Then he went inside?

ANSWER: Well, yes. If you would just let me tell it in my own way, perhaps that would be better.

6 (#1)

QUESTION: You talked to him perhaps five minutes before the door there?
ANSWER: Yes.
QUESTION: And he went in the house. How long did he stay in the house?
ANSWER: Well, that is a little difficult to say.
QUESTION: Did you see him leave the house?
ANSWER: No, I did 8 not.
             X

THE COURT'S CHARGE TO THE JURY

Gentlemen of the jury, it is my custom in charging a jury to stand as counsel have been standing in summing up to you and as counsel rises when it addresses the court, because you gentlemen are now the court. The entire burden and duty in this case now rests on your shoulders. My part of this case has been comparatively small. I had very few technical questions of evidence to rule upon. There were days that passed when I believe there was not a single question raised on questions of evidence. My sole duty is to sit here and keep order and listen to the testimony so that I may properly charge you at the close of this case.

The law involved in this case is quite simple. It is just as simple as might be involved in a contract for building a garage in your backyard. It is, of course, an important case, and the weightiest duty in this case falls on your shoulders. You are the sole judges of the fact. You must determine where the truth in this case lies after I have charged you.

This case drawn out for some days, but I assure you, gentlemen, that it might have been much longer but for the very able work of counsel for both the plaintiff and the defendant in this case, and I wish to compliment them on the way the cases of their clients were presented. I have had cases of this nature before and I might say that never have I heard a case so well presented on either side. I wish also to compliment you gentlemen on your close attention. I realize that it has been a great sacrifice to many of you to be with us for so long. Some of you told me that you were making business sacrifices, but you come to an end of your labors now, or will shortly, and I want to compliment you on the close attention that you have paid to the testimony.

Counsel have very fully summed up their cases. I did not impose any stringent limit on their summation and I feel that the facts are fresh in your minds. It will, of course, be necessary for me to refer from time to time to some of the facts in this case to point the rules of law which I shall give to you. It is necessary in each case to lay before the jury those general principles of law which apply to all cases in a civil court.

In all actions in this court, gentlemen, the law places upon the plaintiff the burden of proving and convincing the jury by a fair preponderance of the credible evidence in the case that he or it is entitled to the verdict it seeks. When we refer to the fair preponderance of the credible evidence we do not mean that the plaintiff must bring in the greater number of witnesses or that it must offer the greater number of exhibits into evidence. We refer entirely to the quality of the testimony of the witnesses, and the quality of the exhibits, and the weight that the exhibits as offered by the parties to the action may have. The mere bringing of an action does not mean, of course, that the plaintiff must recover. You must feel, after having listened to all the testimony, that the plaintiff has convinced you that its version of the case is the correct and proper and truthful version of the case, and that applying the law as I give it to you, the plaintiff is entitled to the verdict that it seeks.

In weighing the testimony you will, of course, take into consideration the character of the testimony of the various witnesses; their interest in the case and, of course, the manner in which they have testified; their qualifications in the event of their testifying as experts; their education, their experience, and all those things which you believe have a bearing on the quality of the testimony and the weight which you believe should be given to it. Take the testimony of all of the witnesses. Take into consideration the facts as they were brought before you by the exhibits.in the case. From that determine where the truth in this case lies; whether or not the plaintiff has sustained the burden of proof to which we have referred. If, after considering all the evidence in the case, you are unable to determine where the truth in this case lies, then the plaintiff has failed to sustain the burden of proof and you must find for the defendant.

Plaintiff alleges that through the. fault of the defendant City of New York the contract which it undertook to execute was not finished within the contract time; that because of its inability to finish in contract time due, it says, to the fault and breach on the part of the City of New York in fulfillment of its covenants that it was damaged due to the fact that after the close of the contract period it was obliged to pay increased prices for both labor and material and that the prolonged use of capital was another item of damage.

PRACTICE AND DRILL IN SHORTHAND OUTLINES
FOR
LEGAL (HEARING/REPORTING) STENOGRAPHERS
(SIMPLIFIED & ANNIVERSARY)

CONTENTS

	Page
A Fortiori ...... Adjudication	1
Advance ...... Appropriation	2
Appurtenant ...... Bench	3
Beneficiary ...... Certiorari	4
Charge ...... Consignee	5
Consignor ...... Criteria (pl.)	6
Damages ...... Deterioration	7
Detriment ...... Duress	8
Easement ...... Evidence	9
Ex Contractu ...... Fiscal	10
Foreclosure (Sale) ...... Guilty	11
Habeas Corpus ...... Indemnify	12
Indemnity ...... Issue	13
Jeopardy ...... Libel	14
Lien ...... Mortgage	15
Mortgagee ...... Nunc Pro Tunc	16
Object ...... Ordinance	17
Parol ...... Preponderance	18
Prima Facie ...... Punitive	19
Quash ...... Remand	20
Replevin ...... Situs	21
Sovereign ...... Syllabus	22
Tenant ...... Unilateral	23
Vacate ...... Writ	24

PRACTICE AND DRILL IN SHORTHAND OUTLINES

FOR

LEGAL STENOGRAPHERS

(SIMPLIFIED & ANNIVERSARY)

	SIMPLIFIED	ANNIVERSARY	
a fortiori			A term meaning you can reason one thing from the existence of certain facts.
a priori			From what goes before.
ab initio			From the beginning.
abate			To diminish or put an end to.
abet			To encourage the commission of a crime.
abeyance			Suspension, temporary suppression.
abide			To accept the consequences of.
abrogate			To annul, repeal, or destroy.
abscond			To hide or absent oneself to avoid legal action.
abstract			A summary.
abut			To border on, to touch.
access			Approach; in real property law it means the right of the owner of property to the use of the highway or road next to his land, without obstruction by intervening property owners.
accessory			In criminal law, it means the person who contributes or aids in the commission of a crime.
accommodated party			One to whom credit is extended on the strength of another person signing a commercial paper.
accommodation paper			A commercial paper to which the accommodating party has put his name.
accomplice			In criminal law, it means a person who together with the principal offender commits a crime.
accord			An agreement to accept something different or less than that to which one is entitled, which extinguishes the entire obligation.
accord and satisfaction			When the agreement (accord) is executed and performed according to its terms.
account			A statement of mutual demands in the nature of debt and credit between parties.
accretion			The act of adding to a thing; in real property law, it means gradual accumulation of land by natural causes.
accrue			To grow to; to be added to.
acquiescence			A silent appearance of consent.
acquit			To legally determine the innocence of one charged with a crime.
ad infinitum			Indefinitely.
ad valorem			According to value.
addendum (sing.) addenda (pl.)			An addition; a supplement to a book.
adjudication			The judgment given in a case.

	SIMPLIFIED	ANNIVERSARY	
advance			In commercial law, it means to pay money or render other value before it is due.
adverse			Opposed; contrary.
advocate			(v.) To speak in favor of; (n.) one who assists, defends, or pleads for another.
affiant			A person who makes and signs an affidavit.
affidavit			A written and sworn to declaration of facts, voluntarily made.
affirm			To ratify; also when an appellate court affirms a judgment, decree, or order, it means that it is valid and right and must stand as rendered in the lower court.
aforementioned aforesaid			Before or already said.
allege			To assert.
allotment			A share or portion.
ambiguity			Uncertainty; capable of being understood in more than one way.
amendment			Any language made or proposed as a change in some principal writing.
amicus curiae			A friend of the court; one who has an interest in a case, although not a party in the case, who volunteers advice upon matters of law to the judge. For example, a brief amicus curiae.

	SIMPLIFIED	ANNIVERSARY	
amortization			To provide for a gradual extinction of (a future obligation) in advance of maturity, especially, by periodical contributions to a sinking fund which will be adequate to discharge a debt or make a replacement when it becomes necessary.
ancillary			Aiding, auxiliary.
annotation			A note added by way of comment or explanation.
answer			A written statement made by a defendant setting forth the grounds of his defense.
ante			Before.
appeal			The removal of a case from a lower court to one of superior jurisdiction for the purposes of obtaining a review.
appearance			Coming into court as a party to a suit.
appellant			The party who takes an appeal from one court or jurisdiction to another (appellate) court for review.
appellee			The party against whom an appeal is taken.
appropriate			To make a thing one's own.
appropriation			Prescribing the destination of a thing; the act of the legislature designating a particular fund, to be applied to some object of government expenditure.

	SIMPLIFIED	ANNIVERSARY	
appurtenant			Belonging to; accessory or incident to.
arbitrary			Unreasoned; not governed by any fixed rules or standard.
arguendo			By way of argument.
assent			A declaration of willingness to do something in compliance with a request.
assert			Declare.
assess			To fix the rate or amount.
assign			To transfer; to appoint; to select for a particular purpose.
assignee			One who receives an assignment.
assignor			One who makes an assignment.
averment			A positive statement of facts.

B

	SIMPLIFIED	ANNIVERSARY	
bail			To obtain the release of a person from legal custody by giving security and promising that he shall appear in court; to deliver (goods, etc.) in trust to a person for a special purpose.
bailment			Delivery of personal property to another to be held for a certain purpose and to be returned when the purpose is accomplished.
bailee			One to whom personal property is delivered under a contract of bailment.
bailor			The party who delivers goods to another, under a contract of bailment.
banc (or bank)			Bench; the place where a court sits permanently or regularly; also the assembly of all the judges of a court.
bankrupt			An insolvent person, technically, one declared to be bankrupt after a bankruptcy proceeding.
bar			The legal profession.
barter			A contract by which parties exchange goods for other goods.
bearer			In commercial law, it means the person in possession of a commercial paper which is payable to the bearer.
bench			The court itself; or the judge.

	SIMPLIFIED	ANNIVERSARY	
beneficiary			A person benefiting under a will, trust, or agreement.
bequest			A gift of personal property under a will.
bill			A formal written statement of complaint to a court of justice; also, a draft of an act of the legislature before it becomes a law; also, accounts for goods sold, services rendered, or work done.
bona fide			In or with good faith; honestly.
bond			An instrument by which the maker promises to pay a sum of money to another, usually providing that upon performance of a certain condition shall be void.
breach			The breaking or violating of a law, or the failure to carry out a duty.
brief			A written document, prepared by a lawyer to serve as the basis of an argument upon a case in court, usually an appellate court.
by-laws			Regulations, ordinances, or rules enacted by a corporation, association, etc., for its own government.

	SIMPLIFIED	ANNIVERSARY	
canon			A doctrine; also, a law or rule, of a church or association in particular.
caption			In a pleading, deposition or other paper connected with a case in court, it is the heading or introductory clause which shows the names of the parties, name of the court, number of the case on the docket or calendar, etc.
carrier			A person or corporation undertaking to transport persons or property.
case			A general term for an action; cause, suit, or controversy before a judicial body.
cause			A suit, litigation or action before a court.
caveat emptor			Let the buyer beware. This term expresses the rule that the purchaser of an article must examine, judge, and test it for himself, being bound to discover any obvious defects or imperfections.
certificate			A written representation that some legal formality has been complied with.
certiorari			To be informed of; the name of a writ issued by a superior court directing the lower court to send up to the former the record and proceedings of a case.

	SIMPLIFIED	ANNIVERSARY	
charge			An obligation or duty; a formal complaint; an instruction of the court to the jury upon a case.
charter			(n.) The authority by virtue of which an organized body acts; (v.) in mercantile law, it means to hire or lease a vehicle or vessel for transportation.
chattel			An article of personal property.
circuit			A division of the country, for the administration of justice; a geographical area served by a court.
citation			The act of the court by which a person is summoned or cited; also, a reference to legal authority.
civil (actions)			It indicates the private rights and remedies of individuals in contrast to the word "criminal" (actions) which relates to prosecution for violation of laws.
claim			(n.) Any demand held or asserted as of right.
codify			To arrange the laws of a country into a code.
cognizance			Notice or knowledge.
collateral			By the side; accompanying; an article or thing given to secure performance of a promise.
comity			Courtesy; the practice by which one court follows the decision of another court on the same question.

	SIMPLIFIED	ANNIVERSARY	
commit			To perform, as an act; to perpetrate, as a crime; to send a person to prison.
common law			As distinguished from law created by the enactment of legislature (called statutory law), it relates to those principles and rules of action which derive their authority solely from usages and customs of immemorial antiquity, particularly with reference to the ancient unwritten law of England. The written pronouncements of the common law are found in court decisions.
complainant			One who applies to the court for legal redress.
complaint			The pleading of a plaintiff in a civil action; or a charge that a person has committed a specified offense.
compromise			An arrangement for settling a dispute by agreement.
concur			To agree, consent.
condition			Mode or state of being; a qualification or restriction.
consign			To give in charge; commit; entrust; to send or transmit goods to a merchant, factor, or agent for sale.
consignee			One to whom a consignment is made.

	SIMPLIFIED	ANNIVERSARY		
consignor			One who sends or makes a consignment.	
conspiracy			In criminal law, it means an agreement between two or more persons to commit an unlawful act.	
conspirators			Persons involved in a conspiracy.	
constitution			The fundamental law of a nation or state.	
constructive			An act or condition assumed from other acts or conditions.	
construe			To ascertain the meaning of language.	
consummate			To complete.	
contiguous			Adjoining; touching; bounded by.	
contingent			Possible, but not assured; dependent upon some condition.	
continuance			The adjournment or postponement of an action pending in a court.	
contra			Against, opposed to; contrary.	
contract			An agreement between two or more persons to do or not to do a particular thing.	
conversion			Dealing with the personal property of another as if it were one's own, without right.	
conveyance			An instrument transferring title to land.	

	SIMPLIFIED	ANNIVERSARY		
conviction			Generally, the result of a criminal trial which ends in a judgment or sentence that the defendant is guilty as charged.	
co-operative (also cooperative)			A cooperative is a voluntary organization of persons with a common interest, formed and operated along democratic lines for the purpose of supplying services at cost to its members and other patrons, who contribute both capital and business.	
corroborate			To strengthen; to add weight by additional evidence.	
counterclaim			A claim presented by a defendant in opposition to or deduction from the claim of the plaintiff.	
county			Political subdivision of a state.	
covenant			Agreement.	
credible			Worthy of belief.	
creditor			A person to whom a debt is owing by another person, called the "debtor".	
criterion (sing.) criteria (pl.)			A means or tests for judging; a standard or standards.	

D

	SIMPLIFIED	ANNIVERSARY	
damages			A monetary compensation, which may be recovered in the courts by any person who has suffered loss, or injury, whether to his person, property or rights through the unlawful act or omission or negligence of another.
de facto			In fact; actually but without legal authority.
de jure			Of right; legitimate; lawful.
de minimis			Very small or trifling.
de novo			Anew; afresh; a second time.
debt			A specified sum of money owing to one person from another, including not only the obligation of the debtor to pay, but the right of the creditor to receive and enforce payment.
decedent			A dead person.
decision			A judgment or decree pronounced by a court in determination of a case.
decree			An order of the court, determining the rights of all parties to a suit.
deed			A writing containing a contract sealed and delivered; particularly to convey real property.
default			The failure to fulfill a duty, observe a promise, discharge an obligation, or perform an agreement.

	SIMPLIFIED	ANNIVERSARY	
defendant			The person defending or denying; the party against whom relief or recovery is sought in an action or suit.
defraud			To practice fraud; to cheat or trick.
delegate			(v.) To entrust to the care or management of another.
demur (v.) demurrer (n.)			(v.) To dispute the sufficiency in law of the pleading of the other side.
demurrage			In maritime law, it means, the sum fixed or allowed as remuneration to the owners of a ship for the detention of their vessel beyond the number of days allowed for loading and unloading or for sailing; also used in railroad terminology.
denial			A form of pleading; refusing to admit the truth of a statement, charge, etc.
deposition			Testimony given under oath outside of court for use in court or for the purpose of obtaining information in preparation for trial of a case.
deponent			One who gives under oath testimony which is reduced to writing.
deterioration			A degeneration such as from decay, corrosion or disintegration.

7

33

	SIMPLIFIED	ANNIVERSARY	
detriment			Any loss or harm to person or property.
deviation			A turning aside.
devise			A gift of real property by the last will and testament of the donor.
dictum (sing.) dicta (pl.)			Any statements made by the court in an opinion concerning some rule of law not necessarily involved nor essential to the determination of the case.
disaffirm			To repudiate.
dismiss			In an action or suit, it means to dispose of the case without any further consideration or hearing.
dissent			To denote disagreement of one or more judges of a court with the decision passed by the majority upon a case before them.
docket			(n.) A formal record, entered in brief, of the proceedings in a court.
doctrine			A rule, principle, theory of law.
domicile			That place where a man has his true, fixed and permanent home to which whenever he is absent he has the intention of returning.
draft			(n.) A commercial paper ordering payment of money drawn by one person on another.
drawee			The person who is requested to pay the money.
drawer			The person who draws the commercial paper and addresses it to the drawee.
duress			Use of force to compel performance or non-performance of an act.

E

	SIMPLIFIED	ANNIVERSARY	
easement			A liberty, privilege, or advantage without profit, in the lands of another.
egress			Act or right of going out or leaving; emergence.
ejusdem generis			Of the same kind, class or nature. A rule used in the construction of language in a legal document.
embezzlement			To steal; to appropriate fraudulently to one's own use property entrusted to one's care.
enact			To make into a law.
endorsement			Act of writing one's name on the back of a note, bill or similar written instrument.
enjoin			To require a person, by writ of injunction from a court of equity, to perform or to abstain or desist from some act.
entirety			The whole; that which the law considers as one whole, and not capable of being divided into parts.
enumerated			Mentioned specifically; designated.
enure			To operate or take effect.
equity			In its broadest sense, this term denotes the spirit and the habit of fairness, justness, and right dealing which regulate the conduct of men.
error			A mistake of law, or the false or irregular application of law as will nullify the judicial proceedings.
escrow			A deed, bond or other written engagement, delivered to a third person, to be delivered by him only upon the performance or fulfillment of some condition.
estate			The interest which any one has in lands, or in any other subject of property.
estop			To stop, bar, or impede.
estoppel			A rule of law which prevents a man from alleging or denying a fact, because of his own previous act.
et al. (alii)			And others.
et seq. (sequentia)			And the following.
et ux. (uxor)			And wife.
evidence			Documents or testimony of witnesses which tend to prove or disprove any matter in question, usually submitted to a jury to enable them to decide.

	SIMPLIFIED	ANNIVERSARY	
ex contractu / ex delicto			In law, rights and causes of action are divided into two classes, those arising *ex contractu* (from a contract) and those arising *ex delicto* (from a delict or tort).
ex officio			From office; by virtue of the office.
ex parte			On one side only; by or for one.
ex post facto			After the fact.
ex rel. (relations)			Upon relation or information.
exception			An objection upon a matter of law to a decision made, either before or after judgment by a court.
executor (male) / executrix (female)			A person who has been appointed by will to execute the will.
executory			That which is yet to be executed or performed.
exempt			To release from some liability to which others are subject.
exoneration			The removal of a burden, charge or duty.

F

	SIMPLIFIED	ANNIVERSARY	
f.a.s.			"Free alongside ship"; delivery at dock for ship named.
f.o.b.			"Free on board"; seller will deliver to car, truck, vessel, or other conveyance by which goods are to be transported, without expense or risk of loss to the buyer or consignee.
fabricate			To construct; to invent a false story.
factor			A commercial agent.
feasance			The doing of an act.
felony			Generally, a criminal offense that may be punished by death or imprisonment for more than one year as differentiated from a misdemeanor.
feme sole			A single woman.
fiduciary			A person who is invested with rights and powers to be exercised for the benefit of another person.
fieri facias			A writ of execution commanding the sheriff to levy and collect the amount of a judgment from the goods and chattels of the judgment debtor.
fiscal			Relating to accounts or the management of revenue.

	SIMPLIFIED	ANNIVERSARY	
foreclosure (sale)			A sale of mortgaged property to obtain satisfaction of the mortgage out of the sale proceeds.
forfeiture			A penalty, a fine.
forgery			Fabricating or producing falsely, counterfeited.
fortuitous			Accidental.
forum			A court of justice; a place of jurisdiction.
fraud			Deception; trickery.
fungible			Of such kind or nature that one specimen or part may be used in the place of another.

G

	SIMPLIFIED	ANNIVERSARY	
garnishment			A legal process to reach the money or effects of a defendant, in the possession or control of a third person.
garnishee			Person garnished.
grant			To agree to; convey, especially real property.
grantee			The person to whom a grant is made.
grantor			The person by whom a grant is made.
gratuitous			Given without a return, compensation or consideration.
guaranty			(n.) A promise to answer for the payment of some debt, or the performance of some duty, in case of the failure of another person, who, in the first instance, is liable for such payment or performance.
guilty			Establishment of the fact that one has committed a breach of conduct; especially a violation of law.

	SIMPLIFIED	ANNIVERSARY	
habeas corpus			You have the body; the name given to a variety of writs, having for their object to bring a party before a court or judge for decision as to whether such person is being lawfully held prisoner.
habendum			In conveyancing; it is the clause in a deed conveying land which defines the extent of ownership to be held by the grantee.
hearing			A proceeding whereby the arguments of the interested parties are heard.
hearsay			A type of testimony given by a witness who relates, not what he knows personally, but what others have told him, or what he has heard said by others.
heir			Generally, one who inherits property, real or personal.
hypothesis			A supposition, assumption, or theory.

	SIMPLIFIED	ANNIVERSARY	
i.e. (Id est)			That is.
ib., or ibid. (ibidem)			In the same place; used to refer to a legal reference previously cited to avoid repeating the entire citation.
illicit			Prohibited; unlawful.
illusory			Deceiving by false appearance.
immunity			Exemption.
impeach			To accuse, to dispute.
impediments			Disabilities, or hindrances.
implead			To sue or prosecute by due course of law.
implied			Not expressly stated; inferential.
imputed			Attributed or charged to.
in toto			In the whole; completely.
inchoate			Imperfect; unfinished.
incompetent			One who is incapable of caring for his own affairs because he is mentally deficient or undeveloped.
incumbrance			Generally a claim, lien, charge or liability attached to and binding real property.
indemnify			To secure against loss or damage; also, to make reimbursement to one for a loss already incurred by him.

	SIMPLIFIED	ANNIVERSARY	
Indemnity			An agreement to reimburse another person in case of an anticipated loss falling upon him.
Indicia			Signs; indications.
Indictment			An accusation in writing found and presented by a grand jury charging that a person has committed a crime.
Indorse			To write a name on the back of a legal paper or document generally, a negotiable instrument.
Information			A formal accusation of crime made by a prosecuting attorney.
infra			Below, under; this word occurring by itself in a publication refers the reader to a future part of the publication.
Ingress			The act of going into.
Injunction			A writ or order by the court requiring a person generally, to do or to refrain from doing an act.
Insolvent			The condition of a person who is unable to pay his debts.
Instruction			A direction given by the judge to the jury concerning the law of the case.
interim			In the meantime; time intervening.

	SIMPLIFIED	ANNIVERSARY	
interlocutory			Temporary, not final; something intervening between the commencement and the end of a suit which decides some point or matter, but is not a final decision of the whole controversy.
interrogatories			A series of formal written questions used in the examination of a party or a witness usually prior to a trial.
intestate			A person who dies without a will.
inure			To result, to take effect.
ipso facto			By the fact itself; by the mere fact.
issue			(n.) The disputed point or question in a case.

J

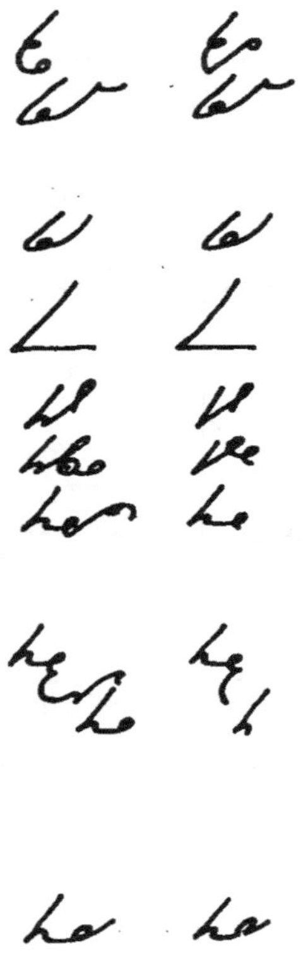

	SIMPLIFIED / ANNIVERSARY	
jeopardy		Danger, hazard, peril.
joinder		Joining; uniting with another person in some legal steps or proceeding.
joint		United; combined.
judgment		The official decision of a court of justice.
judicial or judiciary		Relating to or connected with the administration of justice.
jurisdiction		The authority to hear and determine controversies between parties.
jurisprudence		The philosophy of law.
jury		A body of persons legally selected to inquire into any matter of fact, and to render their verdict according to the evidence.
jurat		The clause written at the foot of an affidavit, stating when, where and before whom such affidavit was sworn.

L

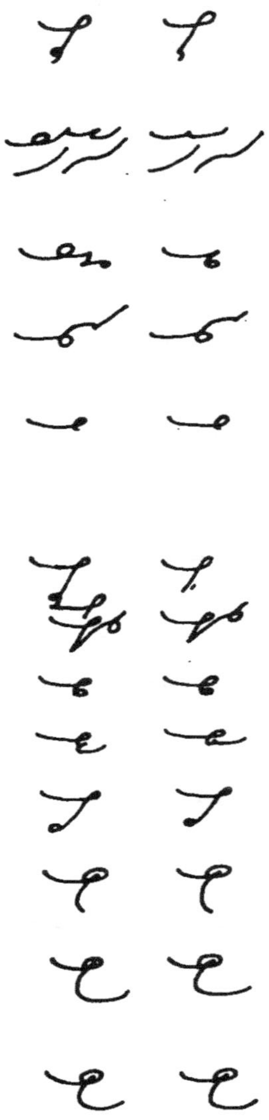

	SIMPLIFIED / ANNIVERSARY	
laches		The failure to diligently assert a right, which results in a refusal to allow relief.
landlord and tenant		A phrase used to denote the legal relation existing between the owner and occupant of real estate.
larceny		Stealing personal property belonging to another.
latent		Hidden; that which does not appear on the face of a thing.
lease		A contract by which one conveys real estate for a limited time usually for a specified rent; personal property also may be leased.
legislation		The act of enacting laws.
legitimate		Lawful.
lessee		One to whom a lease is given.
lessor		One who grants a lease.
levy		A collecting or exacting by authority.
liable		Responsible; bound or obligated in law or equity.
libel		(v.) To defame or injure a person's reputation by a published writing.
libel		(n.) The initial pleading on the part of the plaintiff in an admiralty proceeding.

J

	SIMPLIFIED	ANNIVERSARY	
lien			A hold or claim which one person has upon the property of another as a security for some debt or charge.
liquidated			Fixed; settled.
lis pendens			A pending suit.
literal			According to the language.
litigant			A party to a lawsuit.
litigation			A judicial controversy.
locus			A place.

M

	SIMPLIFIED	ANNIVERSARY	
malice			The doing of a wrongful act intentionally without just cause or excuse.
mandamus			The name of a writ issued by a court to enforce the performance of some public duty.
mandatory			(adj.) Containing a command.
marshaling			Arranging or disposing of in order.
maxim			An established principle or proposition.
ministerial			That which involves obedience to instruction, but demands no special discretion, judgment or skill.
misappropriate			Dealing fraudulently with property entrusted to one.
misdemeanor			A crime less than a felony and punishable by a fine or imprisonment for less than one year.
misrepresentation			An untrue representation of facts.
mitigate			To make or become less severe, harsh.
moot			(adj.) Unsettled, undecided, not necessary to be decided.
mortgage			A conveyance of property upon condition, as security for the payment of a debt or the performance of a duty, and to become void upon payment or performance according to the stipulated terms.

	SIMPLIFIED	ANNIVERSARY	
mortgagee			A person to whom property is mortgaged.
mortgagor			One who gives a mortgage.
motion			In legal proceedings, a "motion" is an application, either written or oral, addressed to the court by a party to an action or a suit requesting the ruling of the court on a matter of law.
mutuality			Reciprocation.

N

	SIMPLIFIED	ANNIVERSARY	
negligence			The failure to exercise that degree of care which an ordinarily prudent person would exercise under like circumstances.
negotiable (instrument)			Any instrument obligating the payment of money which is transferable from one person to another by endorsement and delivery or by delivery only.
negotiate			To transact business; to transfer a negotiable instrument; to seek agreement for the amicable disposition of a controversy or case.
nolle prosequi			A formal entry upon the record, by the plaintiff in a civil suit or the prosecuting officer in a criminal action, by which he declares that he "will no further prosecute" the case.
nolo contendere			The name of a plea in a criminal action, having the same effect as a plea of guilty; but not constituting a direct admission of guilt.
nominal			Not real or substantial.
novation			The substitution of a new debt or obligation for an existing one.
nunc pro tunc			A phrase applied to acts allowed to be done after the time when they should be done, with a retroactive effect.

	SIMPLIFIED	ANNIVERSARY	
order			A rule or regulation; every direction of a court or judge made or entered in writing but not including a judgment.
ordinance			Generally, a rule established by authority; also commonly used to designate the legislative acts of a municipal corporation.

	SIMPLIFIED	ANNIVERSARY	
object			(v.) To oppose as improper or illegal and referring the question of its propriety or legality to the court.
obligation			A legal duty, by which a person is bound to do or not to do a certain thing.
obligee			The person to whom an obligation is owed.
obligor			The person who is to perform the obligation.
offer			(v.) To present for acceptance or rejection.
offer			(n.) A proposal to do a thing, usually a proposal to make a contract.
offset			A deduction.
opinion			The statement by a judge of the decision reached in a case, giving the law as applied to the case and giving reasons for the judgment; also, a belief or view.
option			The exercise of the power of choice; also a privilege existing in one person, for which he has paid money, which gives him the right to buy or sell real or personal property at a given price within a specified time.

	SIMPLIFIED	ANNIVERSARY	
parol			Oral or verbal.
parity			Equality in purchasing power between the farmer and other segments of the economy.
partition			A legal division of real or personal property between one or more owners.
partnership			An association of two or more persons to carry on as co-owners a business for profit.
patent			(adj.) Evident.
patent			(n.) A grant of some privilege, property, or authority, made by the government or sovereign of a country to one or more individuals.
pecuniary			Monetary.
penultimate			Next to the last.
per curiam			A phrase used in the report of a decision to distinguish an opinion of the whole court from an opinion written by any one judge.
per se			In itself; taken alone.
peremptory			Imperative; absolute.
perjury			To lie or state falsely under oath.
perpetuity			Perpetual existence; also the quality or condition of an estate limited so that it will not take effect or vest within the period fixed by law.
personalty			Short term for personal property.
petition			An application in writing for an order of the court, stating the circumstances upon which it is founded and requesting any order or other relief from a court.
plaintiff			A person who brings a court action.
plea			A pleading in a suit or action.
pleadings			Formal allegations made by the parties of their respective claims and defenses, for the judgment of the court.
pledge			A deposit of personal property as a security for the performance of an act.
pledgee			The party to whom goods are delivered in pledge.
pledgor			The party delivering goods in pledge.
plenary			Full; complete.
precept			An order, warrant, or writ issued to an officer or body of officers, commanding him or them to do some act within the scope of his or their powers.
preponderance			Outweighing.

	SIMPLIFIED	ANNIVERSARY	
prima facie			At first sight.
principal			The source of authority or rights; a person primarily liable as differentiated from "principle" as a primary or basic doctrine.
pro rata			Proportionally.
probate			Relating to proof, especially to the proof of wills.
procedure			In law, this term generally denotes rules which are established by the Federal, State or local Governments regarding the types of pleading and courtroom practice which must be followed by the parties involved in a criminal or civil case.
proclamation			A public notice by an official of some order, intended action, or state of facts.
promissory (note)			A promise in writing to pay a specified sum at an expressed time, or on demand, or at sight, to a named person, or to his order, or bearer.
proprietary			(adj.) Relating or pertaining to ownership; usually a single owner.
prosecute			To carry on an action or other judicial proceeding; to proceed against a person criminally.

	SIMPLIFIED	ANNIVERSARY	
proviso			A limitation or condition in a legal instrument.
proximate			Immediate; nearest.
punitive			Relating to punishment.

Q

	SIMPLIFIED	ANNIVERSARY	
quash			To make void.
quasi			As if; as it were.
quid pro quo			Something for something; the giving of one valuable thing for another.
quitclaim			(v.) To release or relinquish claim or title to, especially in deeds to realty.

R

	SIMPLIFIED	ANNIVERSARY	
ratify			To approve and sanction.
realty			A brief term for real property.
rebut			To contradict; to refute, especially by evidence and arguments.
receiver			A person who is appointed by the court to receive, and hold in trust, property in litigation.
reciprocal			Mutual.
recoupment			To keep back or get something which is due; also, it is the right of a defendant to have a deduction from the amount of the plaintiff's damages because the plaintiff has not fulfilled his part of the same contract.
redeem			To release an estate or article from mortgage or pledge by paying the debt for which it stood as security.
referee			A person to whom a cause pending in a court is referred by the court, to take testimony, hear the parties, and report thereon to the court.
referendum			A method of submitting an important legislative or administrative matter to a direct vote of the people.
remand			To send a case back to the lower court from which it came, for further proceedings.

	SIMPLIFIED	ANNIVERSARY	
replevin			An action to recover goods or chattels wrongfully taken or detained.
reply (replication)			Generally, a reply is what the plaintiff or other person who has instituted proceedings says in answer to the defendant's case.
res judicata			A thing judicially acted upon or decided.
rescind (rescission)			To avoid or cancel a contract.
respondent			A defendant in a proceeding in chancery or admiralty; also, the person who contends against the appeal in a case.
restitution			In equity, it is the restoration of both parties to their original condition (when practicable), upon the rescission of a contract for fraud or similar cause.
retroactive (retrospective)			Looking back; effective as of a prior time.
reversed			A term used by appellate courts to indicate that the decision of the lower court in the case before it has been set aside.
revoke			To recall or cancel.
riparian (rights)			The rights of a person owning land containing or bordering on a water course or other body of water, such as lakes and rivers.

S

	SIMPLIFIED	ANNIVERSARY	
sale			A contract whereby the ownership of property is transferred from one person to another for a sum of money or for any consideration.
sanction			A penalty or punishment provided as a means of enforcing obedience to a law; also, an authorization.
satisfaction			The discharge of an obligation by paying a party what is due to him; or what is awarded to him, by the judgment of a court or otherwise.
scienter			Knowingly; also, it is used in pleading to denote the defendant's guilty knowledge.
scintilla			A spark; also the least particle.
security			Indemnification; the term is applied to an obligation, such as a mortgage or deed of trust, given by a debtor to insure the payment or performance of his debt, by furnishing the creditor with a resource to be used in case of the debtor's failure to fulfill the principal obligation.
sentence			The judgment formally pronounced by the court or judge upon the defendant after his conviction in a criminal prosecution.
set-off			A claim or demand which one party in an action credits against the claim of the opposing party.
situs			Location.

	SIMPLIFIED	ANNIVERSARY	
sovereign			A person, body, or state in which independent and supreme authority is vested.
stare decisis			To follow decided cases.
statute			An act of the legislature.
statute of limitation			A statute limiting the time to bring an action after the right of action has arisen.
stay			To hold in abeyance an order of a court.
stipulation			Any agreement made by opposing attorneys regulating any matter incidental to the proceedings or trial.
subordination (agreement)			An agreement making one's rights inferior to or of a lower rank than another's.
subornation			The crime of procuring a person to lie or to make false statements to a court.
subpoena			A writ or order directed to a person, and requiring his attendance at a particular time and place to testify as a witness.
subpoena duces tecum			A subpoena used, not only for the purpose of compelling witnesses to attend in court, but also requiring them to bring with them books or documents which may be in their possession, and which may tend to elucidate the subject matter of the trial.

	SIMPLIFIED	ANNIVERSARY	
subrogation			The substituting of one for another as a creditor, the new creditor succeeding to the former's rights.
subsidy			A government grant to assist a private enterprise deemed advantageous to the public.
suit			Any civil proceeding by a person or persons against another or others in a court of justice by which the plaintiff pursues the remedies afforded him by law.
summons			A notice to a defendant that an action against him has been commenced and requiring him to appear in court and answer the complaint.
supra			Above; this word occurring by itself in a book refers the reader to a previous part of the book.
surety			A person who binds himself for the payment of a sum of money, or for the performance of something else, for another.
surplusage			Extraneous or unnecessary matter.
survivorship			A term used when a person becomes entitled to property by reason of his having survived another person who had an interest in the property.
syllabus			A note prefixed to a report, especially a case, giving a brief statement of the court's ruling on different issues of the case.

T

	SIMPLIFIED	ANNIVERSARY	
tenant	⌒	⌒	One who holds or possesses lands by any kind of right or title; also, one who has the temporary use and occupation of real property owned by another person (landlord), the duration and terms of his tenancy being usually fixed by an instrument called "a lease".
tender	⌒	⌒	An offer of money; an expression of willingness to perform a contract according to its terms.
term			When used with reference to a court, it signifies the period of time during which the court holds a session, usually of several weeks or months duration.
testamentary			Pertaining to a will or the administration of a will.
testator (male) testatrix (female)			One who makes or has made a testament or will.
testify (testimony)			To give evidence under oath as a witness.
to wit			That is to say; namely.
tort			Wrong; injury to the person.
transitory			Passing from place to place.
trial			The examination of a cause, civil or criminal, before a judge who has jurisdiction over it, according to the laws of the land.
trust			A right of property, real or personal, held by one party for the benefit of another.

U

	SIMPLIFIED	ANNIVERSARY	
ultra vires			Acts beyond the scope and power of a corporation, association, etc.
unilateral			One-sided; obligation upon, or act of one party.

	SIMPLIFIED	ANNIVERSARY	
v			
vacate			To set aside; to move out.
variance			A discrepancy or disagreement between two instruments or two aspects of the same case, which by law should be consistent.
vendee			A purchaser or buyer.
vendor			The person who transfers property by sale, particularly real estate; the term "seller" is used more commonly for one who sells personal property.
venue			The place at which an action is tried, generally based on locality or judicial district in which an injury occurred or a material fact happened.
verdict			The formal decision or finding of a jury.
verify			To confirm or substantiate by oath.
vest			To accrue to.
void			Having no legal force or binding effect.

	SIMPLIFIED	ANNIVERSARY	
w			
waiver			The intentional or voluntary relinquishment of a known right.
warrant (warranty)			(v.) To promise that a certain fact or state of facts, in relation to the subject matter, is, or shall be, as it is represented to be.
warrant			(n.) A writ issued by a judge, or other competent authority, addressed to a sheriff, or other officer, requiring him to arrest the person therein named, and bring him before the judge or court, to answer or be examined regarding the offense with which he is charged.
writ			An order or process issued in the name of the sovereign or in the name of a court or judicial officer, commanding the performance or nonperformance of some act.

STENOGRAPHER-TYPIST EXAMINATION
CONTENTS

	Page
THE TYPING TEST	1
How the Test is Given	1
How the Test is Rated	1
How to Construct Additional Tests	2
Exhibit No. 6 Copying From Plain Paper	3
Practice Exercise	3
Test Exercise	4
Exhibit No. 7 Line Key for 5-Minute Typing Test	5
Speed	5
Accuracy	5
Exhibit No. 8 Maximum Number of Errors Permitted on 5-Minute Tests	6
THE DICTATION TEST	7
How the Transcript Booklet Works	7
How the Test is Administered	8
How the Answer Sheet is Scored	8
How to Construct Additional Tests	9
Exhibit No. 9 Dictation Test	11
Practice Dictation	11
Exhibit No. 10 Practice Dictation Transcript Sheet	13
Alphabetic World List	13
Transcript	13
Exhibit No. 11 Transcript Booklet-Dictation Test	15
Directions for Completing the Transcript	15
Directions for Marking the Separate Answer Sheet	15
Word List	16
Transcript	16
Exhibit No. 12 Key (Correct Answers)	18

THE TYPING TEST

In the test of ability to type, the applicant meets a single task, that of copying material exactly as it is presented. He must demonstrate how rapidly he can do so and with what accuracy. A specimen of the typing test is shown as Exhibit No. 6.

How The Test is Given

In order to follow usual examination procedure in giving the test, each competitor will need a copy of the test and two sheets of typewriter paper. About 15 minutes will be needed for the complete typing test.

Three minutes are allowed for reading the instructions on the face of the test and 3 minutes for the practice typing. The practice exercise consists of typing instructions as to spacing, capitalization, etc., and contains a warning that any erasures will be penalized. The practice typing helps make sure that the typewriter is functioning properly.

After the 3 minutes' practice typing, instruct the competitors to put fresh paper in their machines, and to turn the test page over and read the test for 2 minutes. After the 2 minutes, they are instructed to start typing the test. Five minutes are allowed for the test proper.

How the Test is Rated

The exercise must have been typed about once to meet the speed requirement of 40 words a minute. If this speed is not attained, the test is not scored for accuracy. As shown in Exhibit No. 7, a test paper that contains 17 lines meets the minimum speed requirement. Applicants have been instructed to begin and end each line precisely as in the printed test copy. From Exhibit No. 7 it can be quickly determined whether a typing test is to be rated for accuracy and, if so, the greatest number of errors permitted for the lines typed.

The next step is to compare the test paper with the printed test exercise and to mark and charge errors. The basic principles in charging typing errors are as follows:

Charge 1 for each—
- WORD or PUNCTUATION MARK incorrectly typed or in which there is an erasure. (An error in spacing which follows an incorrect word or punctuation mark is not further charged.)
- SERIES of consecutive words omitted, repeated, inserted, transposed, or erased. Charge for errors within such series, but the total charge cannot exceed the number of words.
- LINE or part of line typed over other material, typed with all capitals, or apparently typed with the fingers on the wrong keys.
- Change from the MARGIN where most lines are begun by the applicant or from the PARAGRAPAH INDENTION most frequently used by the applicant.

The typing score used in the official examination reflects both speed and accuracy, with accuracy weighted twice as heavily as speed. Other methods of rating typing often used in schools are based on gross words per minute or net words per minute (usually with not more than a fixed number of errors). Exhibit No. 8 will enable teachers and applicants to calculate typing proficiency in terms of gross words per minute and errors, and to determine whether that proficiency meets the minimum standards of eligibility required in the regular Civil Service examination.

Exhibit No. 8 gives the maximum number of errors permitted at various speeds for three different levels of typing ability. For example, at the minimum acceptable speed of 17 lines, or 40 gross words per minute, 3 errors are permitted for eligibility as GS-2 Clerk Typist or GS-3 Clerk-Stenographer. For GS-3 Clerk-Typist and GS-4 Clerk-Stenographer, and for GS-4 Clerk-Typist and GS-5 Clerk-Stenographer, higher standards of accuracy in relation to speed are reqired.

How to Construct Additional Tests

Here are some of the principal points followed by the examining staff in constructing typing tests so that the various tests will be comparable.

A passage should be subject matter that might reasonably be given a new typist in a government office. All words must be in sufficiently common use to be understood by most high school seniors, and the more difficult words must be dispersed throughout the passage rather than concentrated in one or two sentences. Sentence structure is not complicated. The length of the test exercise in Exhibit No. 6 is typical—21 lines of about 60 strokes each, with a total of about 1,250 strokes.

EXHIBIT NO. 6: COPYING FROM PLAIN COPY
(Part of the Stenographer-Typist Examination)

Read these directions carefully.

A practice exercise appears at the bottom of this sheet, and the test exercise itself is on the following page. First study these directions. Then, when the signal is given, begin to practice by typing the practice exercise below on the paper that has been given you. The examiner will tell you when to stop typing the practice exercise.

In both the practice and the test exercises, *space, paragraph, spell, punctuate, capitalize,* and *begin and end each line* precisely as shown in the exercises.

The examiner will tell you the exact time you will have to make repeated copies of the test exercise. Each time you complete the exercise, simply double space and begin again. If you fill up one side of the paper, turn it over and continue typing on the other side. Keep on typing until told to stop.

Keep in mind that you must meet minimum standards in both speed and accuracy and that, above these standards, accuracy is twice as important as speed. Make no erasures, insertions, or other corrections in this plain-copy test. Since errors are penalized whether or not they are erased or otherwise "corrected," it is best to keep on typing even though you detect an error.

PRACTICE EXERCISE

This practice exercise is similar in form and in difficulty to the one that you will
be required to typewriter for the plain-copy test. You are to space, capitalize,
punctuate, spell, and begin and end each line precisely as in the copy. Make no
erasures, insertions, or other changes in this test because errors will be
penalized even if they are erased or otherwise corrected. Practice typewriting
this material on scratch paper until the examiner tells you to stop, remembering
that for this examination it is more important for you to typewrite accurately than
to typewrite rapidly.

TEST EXERCISE

  Because they have often learned to know types of architecture by decoration, casual observers sometimes fail to realize that the significant part of a structure is not the ornamentation but the body itself. Architecture, because of its close contact with human lives, is peculiarly and intimately governed by climate. For instance, a home built for comfort in the cold and snow of the northern areas of this country would be unbearably warm in a country with weather such as that of Cuba. A Cuban house, with its open court, would prove impossible to heat in a northern winter.
  Since the purpose of architecture is the construction of shelters in which human beings may carry on their numerous activities, the designer must consider not only climatic conditions but also the function of a building. Thus, although the climate of a certain locality requires that an auditorium and a hospital have several features in common, the purposes for which they will be used demand some difference in structure. For centuries builders have first complied with these two requirements and later added whatever ornamentation they wished. Logically, we should see as mere additions, not as basic parts, the details by which we identify architecture.

EACH TIME YOU REACH THIS POINT, DOUBLE SPACE AND BEGIN AGAIN.

EXHIBIT NO. 7: LINE KEY FOR 5-MINUTE TYPING TEST SHOWING MAXIMUM NUMBER OF ERRORS PERMISSIBLE FOR VARIOUS TYPING SPEEDS, AT GRADES GS-2 TYPIST AND GS-3 STENOGRAPHER

SPEED: In the following example, more than 16 lines have been typed for any speed rating. This sample key is constructed on the premise that if the competitor made the first stroke in her final line (even if it was an error), she is given credit for that line in determining the gross words per minute.

ACCURACY: The gross words per minute typed, at any line is the number *outside* the parentheses opposite that line. The numbers *in* the parentheses show the maximum number of errors permitted for that number of gross words per minute typed. The number of errors permitted increases with the speed. (This sample key shows the requirements for GS-2 Typist and GS-3 Stenographer. Exhibit No. 8 shows the standards for higher grades.) If the number of strokes per line were different, this table would have to be altered accordingly.

	Maximum Number of Errors Per Gross Words Per Minute Typed	
	1st Typing of Exercise	2nd Typing of Exercise
Because they have often learned to know types of architec		52(7)
tecture by decoration, casual observers sometimes fail to		54(7)
realize that the significant part of a structure is not the		56(8)
ornamentation but the body itself. Architecture, because		59(8)
of its close contact with human lives, is peculiarly and		61(9)
intimately governed by climate. For instance, a home built		64(9)
for comfort in the cold and snow of the northern areas of		66(10)
this country would be unbearably warm in a country with		68(10)
weather such as that of Cuba. A Cuban house, with its open		71(11)
court, would prove impossible to heat in a northern winter.		73(11)
Since the purpose of architecture is the construction of		76(12)
shelters in which human beings may carry on their numerous		78(12)
activities, the designer must consider not only climatic con-		80(12)[2]
ditions, but also the function of a building. Thus, although		
the climate of a certain locality requires that an auditorium		
and a hospital have several features in common, the purposes		
for which they will be used demand some difference in struc-	40(3)[1]	
ture. For centuries builders have first complied with these	42(4)	
two requirements and later added whatever ornamentation they	44(5)	
wished. Logically, we should see as mere additions, not as	47(6)	
basic parts, the details by which we identify architecture.	49(6)	

---

[1] The minimum rated speed is 40 gross words per minute for typing from printed copy.

[2] Any material typed after 80 gross words per minute (which is considered 100 in speed) is *not* rated for accuracy.

Note: The number of errors shown above must be proportionately increased for tests which are longer than 5 minutes.

EXHIBIT NO. 8: MAXIMUM NUMBER OF ERRORS PERMITTED ON 5-MINUTE TESTS AT VARIOUS SPEEDS FOR TYPING SCORES REQUIRED FOR TYPIST AND STENOGRAPHER POSITIONS

SPEED	MAXIMUM NUMBER OF ERRORS PERMITTED		
Gross Words Per Minute	GS-2 Clerk-Typist GS-3 Clerk-Stenographer	GS-3 Clerk-Typist GS-4 Clerk-Stenographer	GS-4 Clerk-Typist GS-5 Clerk-Stenographer
Under 40	Ineligible	Ineligible	Ineligible
40	3	9	2
41-42	4	4	2
43-44	5	4	2
45-47	6	5	3
48-49	6	5	3
50-52	7	6	4
53-54	7	6	4
55-56	8	7	5
57-59	8	7	5
60-61	9	8	6
62-64	9	8	7
65-66	10	9	7
67-68	10	9	8
69-71	11	10	8
72-73	11	10	9
74-76	12	11	10
77-78	12	11	10
79-80	12	12	10

NOTE: The number of errors shown above must be proportionately increased for tests which are longer than 5 minutes.

THE DICTATION TEST

The dictation test includes a practice dictation and a test exercise, each consisting of 240 words. The rate of dictation is 80 words a minute.

The dictation passages are nontechnical subject matter that might be given a stenographer in a government office. Sentence structure is not complicated and sentences are not extremely long or short. The words average 1.5 syllables in length.

As shown in Exhibit No. 9, each dictation passage is printed with spacing to show the point that the dictator should reach at the end of each 10 seconds in order to maintain an even dictation rate of 80 words a minute. This indication of timing is one device for assisting all examiners to conform to the intended dictation rate. All examiners are also sent instructions for dictating and a sample passage to be used in practicing dictating before the day of the test. By using these devices for securing uniform dictating and by providing alternate dictation passages that are as nearly equal as possible, the Commission can give each applicant a test that is neither harder nor easier than those given others competing for the same jobs.

The test differs from the conventional dictation test in the method of transcribing the notes. The applicant is not required to type a transcript of the notes, but follows a procedure that permits machine scoring of the test. When typewritten transcripts were still required, examiners rated the test by comparing every word of a competitor's paper with the material dictated and charging errors. Fairness to those competing for employment required that comparable errors be penalized equally. Because of the variety of errors and combinations of error that can be made in transcripts, the scoring of typewritten transcripts required considerable training and consumed much time—many months for large nationwide examination. After years of experimentation, a transcript booklet procedure was devised that simplified and speeded the scoring procedure.

Today, rating is decentralized to U.S. Civil Service Commission area offices, and test scores can be furnished quickly and accurately. The transcript booklet makes these improvements possible.

How the Transcript Booklet Works

The transcript booklet (see Exhibit No. 11) gives the stenographer parts of the dictated passage, but leaves blank spaces where many of the words belong. With adequate shorthand notes, the stenographer can readily fit the correct words into the blank spaces, which are numbered 1 through 125. At the left of the printed partial transcript is a list of words, each word with a capital letter A, B, C, or D beside it. Knowing from the notes what word belongs in a blank space, the competitor looks for it among the words in the list. The letter beside the word or phrase in the list is the answer to be marked in the space on the transcript. In the list there are other words that a competitor with inadequate notes might guess belong in that space, but the capital letter beside these words would be an incorrect answer. (Some persons find it helpful to write the word or the shorthand symbol in the blank space before looking for it in the word list. There is no objection to doing this.)

Look, for example, at the Practice Dictation Transcript Sheet, Exhibit No. 10, question 10. The word dictated is "physical"; it is in the word list with a capital "D." In the transcript, blank number 10 should be answered "D."

None of the words in the list is marked "E." This is because the answer "E" is reserved for any question when the word dictated for that spot does not appear in the list. Every transcript booklet has spots for which the list does not include the correct words. This provision reduces the possibility that competitors may guess correct answers.

After the stenographer has written the letter of the missing word or phrase in each numbered blank of the transcript, he transfers the answers to the proper spaces on the answer sheet. Directions for marking the separate answer sheet are given on page 1 of Exhibit No. 11.

This transcription procedure should not cause any good stenographer to make a poor showing on the examination. To this end, illustrations of the procedure are included in a sheet of samples that is mailed to each applicant with the notice of when and where to report for examination. Again in the examination room, the applicant uses such a transcript on the practice dictation before the actual dictation is given. A major objective in preparing this publication is to further insure that each prospective competitor is made to feel at ease about using this method of handling how good the notes are.

Use of the transcript booklet and transfer of answers to the answer sheet are clerical tasks that are not part of transcribing by typewriter. Most stenographic positions involve clerical duties for some percentage of the time and it is reasonable, therefore, to include clerical tasks in the examination. Although some unsuccessful competitors for stenographic positions attribute their failure to the use of transcript booklets, analysis of many test papers, notes, and transcripts has shown the frequency of clerical error in this test to be negligible.

How the Test is Administered

Each competitor will need a copy of the Practice Dictation Transcript Sheet (Exhibit No. 10), a copy of the Transcript Booklet (Exhibit No. 11), and an answer sheet (Exhibit No. 2). These should be distributed at the times indicated below.

The Practice Dictation of Exhibit No. 9 should be dictated at the rate indicated by the 10 second divisions in which it is printed. This will be at the rate of 80 words a minute. Then each competitor should be given a copy of the Practice Dictation Transcript Sheet and allowed 7 minutes to study the instructions and to transcribe part of the practice dictation.

The text exercise (reverse of Exhibit No. 9) should also be dictated at the rate of 80 words a minute, for 3 minutes. Each competitor should be given a Transcript Booklet and an answer sheet. He should be told that he will have 3 minutes for reading the directions on the face page, followed by 30 minutes for writing answers in the blank spaces, and then 10 minutes for transferring his answers to the answer sheet. These time limits are those used in the official examination and have been found ample.

How the Answer Sheet is Scored

The correct answers for the test are given in Exhibit No. 12. A scoring stencil may be prepared by copying these answers on a blank answer sheet and then punching out the marked answer boxes. Directions for using the scoring stencil are given at the top of Exhibit No. 12.

In some rare instances where the typewritten transcript is still used, the passing standard on the total transcript is 24 or fewer errors for GS-3 Clerk-Stenographer, and 12 or fewer errors for GS-4. Comparable standards on the parts of the dictation measured by the machine-scored method of transcription are 14 or fewer errors for GS-3, and 6 or fewer errors for GS-4 positions.

A stenographer who can take dictation at 80 words a minute with this degree of accuracy is considered fully qualified. Positions such as Reporting Stenographer and Shorthand Reporter require ability to take dictation at much higher speeds. The test for Reporting Stenographer is dictated at 120 words a minute. Two rates of dictation, 160 and 175 words a minute, are used for the Shorthand Reporter tests for different grade levels.

How to Construct Additional Tests

A teacher who has examined students by the tests in this part may wish to re-examine some of them after a period of further training. For this purpose, it is desirable to use new tests rather than to repeat the same test too often. If additional test material is needed, it should be constructed in accordance with the following principles in order to keep alternative tests comparable.

As already indicated, the subject matter and the vocabulary should not be technical or too unusual; they should appear to be part of the day-to-day business of an efficient government office. In view of the broad range of activities of Federal agencies, this restriction still allows a wide range of subject matter.

For 3 minutes of dictation at 80 words a minute, the exercise should contain 240 words. The average number of syllables should be about 1.5. Sentences should be straightforward, rather than of complicated grammatical construction. At the same time, they should not be short and choppy.

Before the transcript booklet is made, a skeleton transcript should be prepared. One way of beginning is to choose words and groups of words that should be tested. A total of about 140 words of the complete dictation passage should be chosen for testing, since some of the 125 numbered blank spaces in the transcript booklet should represent more than one word. As shown in the transcripts in Exhibits No. 10 and 11, the words selected for testing are not chosen simply by taking every other word; rather, they are single words or series of words distributed throughout the dictation passage. The first word of any sentence should not be used as a test word.

The dictation passage should be divided into four sections of about equal length with a section always breaking at the end of a sentence. A worksheet similar to that shown below should be prepared for each section.

For illustration of the next steps, look at the reverse side of the Practice Dictation Transcript Sheet, Exhibit No. 10; let the two sentences at the bottom of that page represent the dictation. The words that have been chosen for testing are "bring," "about," "to visit," "their," and so on; these words or phrases have been numbered 16, 17, etc. For a convenient worksheet, ruled paper can be divided into columns headed A, B, C, D, and E. Now the words chosen for the blanks should be distributed at random in the various columns. At this point the worksheet for this part of the test will look like the following:

	A	B	C	D	E
16	bring				
17					about
18		to visit			
19				their	
20				to discuss	
21					treatment
22			correction		
23					value
24		see			
25	is not				

(and so on)

Next, think of several plausible errors for each of the blanks; that is, a word beginning with the same sound, a word that fits the preceding or the following word almost as a cliché, etc. Avoid any error that is too conspicuously wrong or too clearly a misfit with printed auxiliaries or articles to present any difficulty. Place each plausible error in column A, B, C, or D of the worksheet, *avoiding* the column that contains the *answer*. The worksheet will now look like the columns below.

Experience will bring out situations that must be avoided, such as use of the same word in more than one column.

Each word in columns A, B, C, and D takes the letter at the head of the column. The words in these columns are grouped in alphabetic order to become the "Word List" for the section of the transcript covered by this worksheet. Since instructions provide that E is to be selected when the exact answer is not listed, the words in column E are NOT included in the "Word List." The sentences are presented with numbered blanks as the "Transcript."

	A	B	C	D	E
16	bring	promote	discuss	understand	
17	all				about
18	visit	to visit	at	during	
19	(all)		young	their	
20	to discover	undertake	{to endorse {indicated	to discuss	
21	treatments				treatment
22	reducing	collection	correction	recognizing	
23	friend	volume		virtue	value
24	know	see	say	satisfied	
25	is not	is	soon	{knows {insisted	

(and so on)

EXHIBIT NO. 9: DICTATION TEST
(Part of the Stenographer-Typist Examination)

PRACTICE DICTATION

INSTRUCTIONS TO THE EXAMINER: This Practice Dictation and one exercise will be dictated at the rate of 80 words a minute. Do not dictate the punctuation except for periods, but dictate with the expression that the punctuation indicates. Use a watch with a second hand to enable you to read the exercises at the proper speed.

Exactly on a minute, start dictating.

	Finish reading each two lines at the number of seconds indicated below.
I realize that this practice dictation is not a part of the examination	10
proper and is not to be scored. (Period) The work of preventing and correcting	20
physical defects in children is becoming more effective as a result of a change	30
in the attitude of many parents. (Period) In order to bring about this change	40
mothers have been invited to visit the schools when their children are being examined	50
and to discuss the treatment necessary for the correction of defects. (Period)	1 min.
There is a distinct value in having a mother see that her child is not the	10
only one who needs attention. (Period) Otherwise a few parents might feel that they	20
were being criticized by having the defects of their children singled out for medical	30
treatment. (Period) The special classes that have been set up have shown the value of	40
the scientific knowledge that has been applied in the treatment of children. (Period)	50
In these classes the children have been taught to exercise by a trained teacher	2 min.
under medical supervision. (Period) The hours of the school day have been divided	10
between school work and physical activity that helps not only to correct their defects	20
but also to improve their general physical condition. (Period) This method of treatment	30
has been found to be very effective except for those who have severe medical	40
defects. (Period) Most parents now see how desirable it is to have these classes	50
that have been set up in the regular school system to meet special needs. (Period)	3 min.

After dictating the practice, pause for 15 seconds to permit competitors to complete their notes. Then continue in accordance with the directions for conducting the examination.

After the Practice Dictation Transcript has been completed, dictate the test from the following.

Exactly on a minute, start dictating.

	Finish reading each two lines at the number of seconds indicated below.
The number enrolled in shorthand classes in the high schools has shown a marked increase. (Period)	10
Today this subject is one of the most popular offered in the field of	20
business education. (Period) When shorthand was first taught, educators claimed that it was of	30
value mainly in sharpening the powers of observation and discrimination. (Period)	40
However, with the growth of business and the increased demand for office workers,	50
educators have come to realize the importance of stenography as a vocational	1 min.
tool. (Period) With the differences in the aims of instruction came changes in	10
the grade placement of the subject. (Period) The prevailing thought has always been that it	20
should be offered in high school. (Period) When the junior high school first came into	30
being, shorthand was moved down to that level with little change in the manner in which	40
the subject was taught. (Period) It was soon realized that shorthand had no place there	50
because the training had lost its vocational utility by the time the student could	2 min.
graduate. (Period) Moreover, surveys of those with education only through junior	10
high school seldom found them at work as stenographers. (Period) For this reason, shorthand	20
was returned to the high school level and is offered as near as possible to the time	30
of graduation so that the skill will be retained when the student takes a job. (Period)	40
Because the age at which students enter office jobs has advanced, there is now	50
a tendency to upgrade business education into the junior college. (Period)	3 min.

After completing the dictation, pause of 15 seconds.
Give a Transcript to each competitor.

EXHIBIT NO. 10: PRACTICE DICTATION TRANSCRIPT SHEET
(Part of the Stenographer-Typist Examination)

The transcript below is part of the material that was dictated to you for practice, except that many of the words have been left out. From your notes, you are to tell what the missing words are. Proceed as follows:

Compare your notes with the transcript and, when you come to a blank in the transcript, decide what word or words belong there. For example, you will find that the word "practice" belongs in blank number 1. Look at the Word List to see whether you can find the same word there. Notice what letter (A, B, C, or D) is printed beside it, and write that letter in the blank. For example, the word "practice" is listed, followed by the letter "B." We have already written "B" in blank number 1 to show you how you are to record your choice. Now decide what belongs in each of the other blanks. (You may also write the word or words, or the shorthand for them, if you wish.) The same word may belong in more than one blank. If the exact answer is not listed, write "E" in the blank.

TRANSCRIPT

I realize that this __B__ dictation is ____
                              1   2

a ____ of the ____ ____ and is ____ ____
   3   4   5   6   7

scored.

    The work of ____ and ____ ____ defects in
                         8   9   10

____ is becoming more ____ as a ____ a
11   12   13

change in the ____ of many ____ ....
                14   15

ALPHABETIC WORD LIST	
about-B	paper-B
against-C	parents-B
attitude-A	part-C
being-D	physical-D
childhood-B	portion-D
children-A	practical-A
correcting-C	practice-B
doctors-B	preliminary-D
effective-D	preventing-B
efficient-A	procedure-A
examination-A	proper-C
examining-C	reason for-A
for-B	result-B
health-B	result of-C
mothers-C	schools-C
never-C	to be-C
not-D	to prevent-A

Each numbered blank in the Transcript is a question. You will be given a separate answer sheet like the sample here, to which you will transfer your answers. The answer sheet has a numbered row of boxes for each question. The answer for blank number 1 is "B." We have already transferred this to number 1 in the Sample Answer Sheet, by darkening the box under "B."

Now transfer your answer for each of questions 2 through 15 to the answer sheet. That is, beside each number on the answer sheet find the letter that is the same as the letter you wrote in the blank with the same number in the transcript, and darken the box below that letter.

After you have marked 15, continue with blank number 16 on the next page WITHOUT WAITING FOR A SIGNAL.

Sample Answer Sheet

	A	B	C	D	E
1		▮			
2					
3					
4					
5					
6					
7					
8					

Sample Answer Sheet (Continued)

	A	B	C	D	E
9					
10					
11					
12					
13					
14					
15					

TRANSCRIPT (continued)

In order to _____ _____ this change, mothers
              16   17
have been invited _____ the schools when _____
                       18   19
children are being examined and _____ the _____
                                    20   21
necessary for the _____ of defects. There is a
                      22
distinct _____ in having a mother _____ that her
         23   24
child _____ the only one who needs attention….
      25

ALPHABETIC WORD LIST	
all-A	reducing-A
at-C	satisfied-D
bring-A	say-C
collection-B	see-B
correction-C	soon-C
discuss-C	their-D
during-D	to discover-A
friend-A	to discuss-D
indicated-C	to endorse-C
insisted-D	to visit-B
is-B	treatments-A
is not-A	understand-D
know-A	undertake-B
knows-D	virtue-D
needed-B	visit-A
promote-B	volume-B
recognizing-D	young-C

Your notes should show that the word "bring" goes in blank 16, and "about" in blank 17. But "about" is *not in the list*; so "E" should be your answer for Question 17.

The two words, "to visit-B," are needed for 18, and the one word "visit-A," would be an incorrect answer.

Fold this page so that the Correct Answers to Samples 1 through 8, below, will lie beside the Sample Answer Sheet you marked for those questions. Compare your answers with the correct answers. Then fold the page and compare the correct answers with your answers for 9 through 15. If one of your answers does not agree with the correct answer, again compare your notes with the samples and make certain you understand the instructions. The correct answers for 16 through 25 are as follows: 16-A, 17-E, 18-B, 19-D, 20-D, 21-E, 22-C, 23-E, 24-B, and 25-A.

For the actual test, you will use a separate answer sheet. As scoring will be done by an electronic scoring machine, it is important that you follow directions carefully. Use a medium No. 2 pencil. You must keep your mark for a question within the box. If you have to erase a mark, be sure to erase it completely. Mark only one answer for each question.

For any stenographer who missed the practice dictation, part of it is given below:

"I realize that this practice dictation is not a part of the examination proper and is not to be scored.

"The work of preventing and correcting physical defects in children is becoming more effective as a result of a change in the attitude of many parents. In order to bring about this change, mothers have been invited to visit the schools when their children are being examined and to discuss the treatment necessary for the correction of defects. There is a distinct value in having a mother see that her child is not the only one who needs attention…"

EXHIBIT NO. 11: TRANSCRIPT BOOKLET – DICTATION TEST
(Part of Stenographer-Typist Examination)

Directions for Completing the Transcript

A transcript of the dictation you have just taken is given on Pages 15 and 16. As in the transcript for the practice dictation, there are numbered blank spaces for many of the words that were dictated. You are to compare your notes with the transcript and, when you come to a blank, decide what word or words belong there. For most of the blanks the words are included in the list beside the transcript; each is followed by a letter, A, B, C, or D. To show that you know which word or words belong in each blank space, you are to write the letter in the blank. You are to write E if the exact answer is NOT listed. (In addition, you may write the word or words, or the shorthand for them, if you wish.) The same choice may belong in more than one blank.

After you have compared your notes with the transcript and have chosen the answer for each blank space, you will be given additional time to transfer your answers to a separate answer sheet.

Directions for Marking the Separate Answer Sheet

On the answer sheet, each question number stands for the blank with the same number in the transcript. For each number, you are to darken the box below the letter that is the same as the letter you wrote in the transcript. (The answers in this booklet will not be rated.) Be sure to use your pencil and record your answers on the separate answer sheet. You must keep your mark within the bod. If you have to erase a mark, be sure to erase it completely. Make only one mark for each question.

Work quickly so that you will be able to finish in the time allowed. First, you should darken the boxes on the answer sheet for the blanks you have lettered. You may continue to use your notes if you have not finished writing letters in the blanks in the transcript, or if you wish to make sure you have lettered them correctly.

TRANSCRIPT

The number _____ in shorthand _____ _____
                   1   2   3
high schools has _____ a _____ _____. Today _____
                4   5   6   7
_____ is one of the most _____ _____ _____ _____ of
  8   9   10   11   12
business _____. When _____ _____ _____ _____
           13   14   15   16   17
educators _____ that it _____ _____ _____ in _____
          18   19   20   21   22
_____ _____ of _____ and _____.
 23   24   25   26

ALPHABETIC WORD LIST	
Write E if the answer is NOT listed	
administration-C	observation-B
along the-B	observing-A
area-A	offered-C
at first-A	of value-C
claimed-C	open-A
classes-B	popular-B
concluded-D	power-B
could be-D	powers-D
courses-C	practical-A
decrease-D	shaping-A
discriminating-C	sharpen-B
discrimination-D	shorthand-D
education-B	shown-C
enrolled-D	stenography-B
entering-A	study-C
field-D	subject-A
first-D	taught-D
given-B	that-C
great-C	the-D
increase-A	these-B
in the-D	this-A
known-D	thought-B
line-C	to be-A
mainly-B	training-D
marked-B	valuable-A
mostly-D	vast-A

...However, _____ the growth of _____ and the _____
                 27   28   29
for _____ _____, _____ have _____ _____ the _____
     30   31   32   33   34   35
of _____ _____ _____ _____ in the _____ _____ of the
    36   37   38   39   40   41
_____. The _____ _____ _____ _____ that _____
 42   43   44   45   46   47
_____ _____ in _____.
  48   49   50

ALPHABETIC WORD LIST	
Write E if the answer is NOT listed	
a change-D	offered-C
administration-C	office-A
aims-A	official-C
always been-A	often been-B
begun-D	ought to be-B
businesses-A	place-B
came-D	placement-D
changes-B	prevailing-B
come-C	rule-D
defects-B	schools-D
demand-B	shorthand-D
demands-A	should be-A
differences-D	significance-C
education-B	stenography-B
educators-D	study-A
for-D	subject-A
given-B	thinking-C
grade-C	this-A
grading-B	thought-B
has-C	tool-B
had-B	to realize-B
have come-A	to recognize-B
high school-B	valuable-A
increased-D	vocational-C
increasing-C	when the-D
institutions-D	with-A
instruction-C	without-C
it-B	workers-C

...When the ____ school ____ ____ ____ ____, ____
         57   58   59   60   61
was ____ to ____ ____ with ____ ____ in ____
    62   63   64   65   66   67
____ ____ the ____ was ____. It was ____
68   69   70   71   72
____ that ____ ____ place ____ ____ the ____
73   74   75   76   77   78
had ____ ____ ____ ____ by the ____ the
    79   80   81   82   83
____ ____ ____ .
84   85   86

ALPHABETIC WORD LIST	
Write E if the answer is NOT listed	
became-B	moved-C
because-B	moved down-B
came-D	occupational-B
change-A	recognized-A
changed-C	shorthand-D
could-C	since-C
could be-D	soon-C
date-D	stenography-B
first-D	student-A
graduate-D	students-C
graduated-B	study-C
had little-C	subject-A
had no-A	taught-D
here-D	that-C
high-C	the-D
into being-A	their-B
into business-C	there-B
junior high-D	this-A
less-B	time-B
lessened-C	training-D
level-C	usefulness-B
little-A	utility-C
lost-D	vocational-C
manner-B	which-A
method-C	

...Moreover, ____ of ____ with ____ ____ ____
            87   88   89   90   91
____ school ____ ____ them ____ as ____. For
92   93   94   95   96
____ ____, shorthand was ____ to the ____ ____ ____
97   98   99   100 101
and is ____ as ____ ____ to the ____ ____ ____
       102   103 104   105 106 107
____ the skill ____ ____ ____ ____ the student
108   109 110 111 112
____ a ____ . Because the ____ ____ students
113   114   115 116
____ office ____ ____ ____, there is ____ a
117   118 119 120   121
____ to ____ ____ education ____ the junior
122   123 124   125
college.

ALPHABETIC WORD LIST	
Write E if the answer is NOT listed	
advanced-A	reason-B
age-A	reasons-D
as far as-C	retained-B
at which-D	school-A
at work-A	secretaries-D
be-B	secures-D
date-D	seldom-C
education-B	showed-A
enter-D	so-A
found-D	stenographers-C
graduating-A	studies-B
graduation-C	surveys-A
has-C	takes-A
high school-B	taught-D
in-A	tendency-B
in order-D	that-C
increased-D	there-B
into-B	this-A
job-B	through-D
junior high-D	time-B
level-C	training-D
may be-C	undertake-A
near as-A	until-A
nearly as-C	upgrade-D
offered-C	when-C
often-B	which-A
only-B	will-B
possible-D	would-D
rarely-D	working-B

KEY (CORRECT ANSWERS)

EXHIBIT NO. 12: SCORING STENCIL-RIGHT ANSWERS

If the competitor marked more than one answer to any question, draw a line through the answer boxes for the question. To make a stencil, punch out the answers on this page or on a separate answer sheet. Place this punched key over a competitor's sheet. Count the right answers. DO NOT GIVE CREDIT FOR DOUBLE ANSWERS.

EXAMINATION SECTION
TEST 1

DIRECTIONS: Each question or incomplete statement is followed by several suggested answers or completions. Select the one that BEST answers the question or completes the statement. *PRINT THE LETTER OF THE CORRECT ANSWER IN THE SPACE AT THE RIGHT.*

Questions 1-6.

DIRECTIONS: Questions 1 through 6 consist of descriptions of material to which a filing designation must be assigned.

Assume that the matters and cases described in the questions were referred for handling to a government legal office which has its files set up according to these file designations. The file designation consists of a number of characters and punctuation marks as described below.

The first character refers to agencies whose legal work is handled by this office. These agencies are numbered consecutively in the order in which they first submit a matter for attention, and are identified in an alphabetical card index. To date numbers have been assigned to agencies as follows:

```
Department of Correction .......................................................... 1
Police Department .................................................................... 2
Department of Traffic ................................................................ 3
Department of Consumer Affairs............................................... 4
Commission on Human Rights .................................................. 5
Board of Elections ..................................................................... 6
Department of Personnel........................................................... 7
Board of Estimate ...................................................................... 8
```

The second character is separated from the first character by a dash. The second character is the last digit of the year in which a particular lawsuit or matter is referred to the legal office.

The third character is separated from the second character by a colon and may consist of either of the following:

I. *A sub-number assigned to each lawsuit to which the agency is a party. Lawsuits are numbered consecutively regardless of year. (Lawsuits are brought by or against agency heads rather than agencies themselves, but references are made to agencies for the purpose of simplification.)*

or II. *A capital letter assigned to each matter other than a lawsuit according to subject, the subject being identified in an alphabetical index. To date, letters have been assigned to subjects as follows:*

```
Citizenship ..................... A        Housing ........................... E
Discrimination ................ B        Gambling ......................... F
Residence Requirements ........ C        Freedom of Religion ........ G
Civil Service Examinations ..... D
```

2 (#1)

These referrals are numbered consecutively regardless of year. The first referral by a particular agency on citizenship, for example, would be designated A1, followed by A2, A3, etc.

If no reference is made in a question as to how many letters involving a certain subject or how many lawsuits have been referred by an agency, assume that it is the first.

For each question, choose the file designation which is MOST appropriate for filing the material described in the question.

1. In January 2010, two candidates in a 2009 civil service examination for positions with the Department of Correction filed a suit against the Department of Personnel seeking to set aside an educational requirement for the title.
The Department of Personnel immediately referred the lawsuit to the legal office for handling.

    A. 1-9:1   B. 1-0:D1   C. 7-9:D1   D. 7-0:1

2. In 2014, the Police Department made its sixth request for an opinion on whether an employee assignment proposed for 2015 could be considered discriminatory.

    A. 2-5:1-B6   B. 2-4:6   C. 2-4:1-B6   D. 2-4:B6

3. In 2015, a lawsuit was brought by the Bay Island Action Committee against the Board of Estimate in which the plaintiff sought withdrawal of approval of housing for the elderly in the Bay Island area given by the Board in 2015.

    A. 8-3:1   B. 8-5:1   C. 8-3:B1   D. 8-5:E1

4. In December 2014, community leaders asked the Police Department to ban outdoor meetings of a religious group on the grounds that the meetings were disrupting the area. Such meetings had been held from time to time during 2014. On January 31, 2015, the Police Department asked the government legal office for an opinion on whether granting this request would violate the worshippers' right to freedom of religion.

    A. 2-4:G-1   B. 2-5:G1   C. 2-5:B-1   D. 2-4:B1

5. In 2014, a woman filed suit against the Board of Elections. She alleged that she had not been permitted to vote at her usual polling place in the 2013 election and had been told she was not registered there. She claimed that she had always voted there and that her record card had been lost. This was the fourth case of its type for this agency.

    A. 6-4:4   B. 6-3:C4   C. 3-4:6   D. 6-3:4

6. A lawsuit was brought in 2011 by the Ace Pinball Machine Company against the Commissioner of Consumer Affairs. The lawsuit contested an ordinance which banned the use of pinball machines on the ground that they are gambling devices.
This was the third lawsuit to which the Department of Consumer Affairs was a party.

    A. 4-1:1   B. 4-3:F1   C. 4-1:3   D. 3F-4:1

7. You are instructed by your supervisor to type a statement that must be signed by the person making the statement and by three witnesses to the signature. The typed statement will take two pages and will leave no room for signatures if the normal margin is maintained at the bottom of the second page.
In this situation, the PREFERRED method is to type

   A. the signature lines below the normal margin on the second page
   B. nothing further and have the witnesses sign without a typed signature line
   C. the signature lines on a third page
   D. some of the text and the signature lines on a third page

8. Certain legal documents always begin with a statement of venue - that is, the county and state in which the document is executed. This is usually boxed with a parentheses or colons.
The one of the following documents that ALWAYS bears a statement of venue in a prominent position at its head is a(n)

   A. affidavit
   B. memorandum of law
   C. contract of sale
   D. will

9. A court stenographer is to take stenographic notes and transcribe the statements of a person under oath. The person has a heavy accent and speaks in ungrammatical and broken English.
When he or she is transcribing the testimony, of the following, the BEST thing for them to do is to

   A. transcribe the testimony exactly as spoken, making no grammatical changes
   B. make only the grammatical changes which would clarify the client's statements
   C. make all grammatical changes so that the testimony is in standard English form
   D. ask the client's permission before making any grammatical changes

10. When the material typed on a printed form does not fill the space provided, a Z-ruling is frequently drawn to fill up the unused space.
The MAIN purpose of this practice is to

    A. make the document more pleasing to the eye
    B. indicate that the preceding material is correct
    C. insure that the document is not altered
    D. show that the lawyer has read it

11. After you had typed an original and five copies of a certain document, some changes were made in ink on the original and were initialed by all the parties. The original was signed by all the parties, and the signatures were notarized.
Which of the following should *generally* be typed on the copies BEFORE filing the original and the copies? The inked changes

    A. but not the signatures, initials, or notarial data
    B. the signatures and the initials but not the notarial data
    C. and the notarial data but not the signatures or initials
    D. the signatures, the initials, and the notarial data

12. The first paragraph of a noncourt agreement *generally* contains all of the following EXCEPT the

    A. specific terms of the agreement
    B. date of the agreement
    C. purpose of the agreement
    D. names of the parties involved

13. When typing an answer in a court proceeding, the place where the word ANSWER should be typed on the first page of the document is

    A. at the upper left-hand corner
    B. below the index number and to the right of the box containing the names of the parties to the action
    C. above the index number and to the right of the box containing the names of the parties to the action
    D. to the left of the names of the attorneys for the defendant

14. Which one of the following statements BEST describes the legal document called an acknowledgment?
    It is

    A. an answer to an affidavit
    B. a receipt issued by the court when a document is filed
    C. proof of service of a summons
    D. a declaration that a signature is valid

15. Suppose you typed the original and three copies of a legal document which was dictated by an attorney in your office. He has already signed the original copy, and corrections have been made on all copies.
    Regarding the copies, which one of the following procedures is the PROPER one to follow?

    A. Leave the signature line blank on the copies
    B. Ask the attorney to sign the copies
    C. Print or type the attorney's name on the signature line on the copies
    D. Sign your name to the copies followed by the attorney's initials

16. Suppose your office is defending a particular person in a court action. This person comes to the office and asks to see some of the lawyer's working papers in his file. The lawyer assigned to the case is out of the office at the time.
    You SHOULD

    A. permit him to examine his entire file as long as he does not remove any materials from it
    B. make an appointment for the caller to come back later when the lawyer will be there
    C. ask him what working papers he wants to see and show him only those papers
    D. tell him that he needs written permission from the lawyer in order to see any records

17. Suppose that you receive a phone call from an official who is annoyed about a letter from your office which she just received. The lawyer who dictated the letter is not in the office at the moment.
Of the following, the BEST action for you to take is to

    A. explain that the lawyer is out but that you will ask the lawyer to return her call when he returns
    B. take down all of the details of her complaint and tell her that you will get back to her with an explanation
    C. refer to the proper file so that you can give her an explanation of the reasons for the letter over the phone
    D. make an appointment for her to stop by the office to speak with the lawyer

18. Suppose that you have taken dictation for an interoffice memorandum. You are asked to prepare it for distribution to four lawyers in your department whose names are given to you. You will type an original and make four copies. Which one of the following is CORRECT with regard to the typing of the lawyers' names?
The names of all of the lawyers should appear

    A. *only* on the original
    B. on the original and each copy should have the name of one lawyer
    C. on each of the copies but not on the original
    D. on the original and on all of the copies

19. Regarding the correct typing of punctuation, the GENERALLY accepted practice is that there should be

    A. two spaces after a semi-colon
    B. one space before an apostrophe used in the body of a word
    C. no space between parentheses and the matter enclosed
    D. one space before and after a hyphen

20. Suppose you have just completed typing an original and two copies of a letter requesting information. The original is to be signed by a lawyer in your office. The first copy is for the files, and the second is to be used as a reminder to follow up.
The PROPER time to file the file copy of the letter is

    A. after the letter has been signed and corrections have been made on the copies
    B. before you take the letter to the lawyer for his signature
    C. after a follow-up letter has been sent
    D. after a response to the letter has been received

21. A secretary in a legal office has just typed a letter. She has typed the copy distribution notation on the copies to indicate *blind copy distribution*. This *blind copy* notation shows that

    A. copies of the letter are being sent to persons that the addressee does not know
    B. copies of the letter are being sent to other persons without the addressee's knowledge
    C. a copy of the letter will be enlarged for a legally blind person
    D. a copy of the letter is being given as an extra copy to the addressee

22. Suppose that one of the attorneys in your office dictates material to you without indicating punctuation. He has asked that you give him, as soon as possible, a single copy of a rough draft to be triple-spaced so that he can make corrections.
Of the following, what is the BEST thing for you to do in this situation?

    A. Assume that no punctuation is desired in the material
    B. Insert the punctuation as you type the rough draft
    C. Transcribe the material exactly as dictated, but attach a note to the attorney stating your suggested changes
    D. Before you start to type the draft, tell the attorney you want to read back your notes so that he can indicate punctuation

23. When it is necessary to type a mailing notation such as CERTIFIED, REGISTERED, or FEDEX on an envelope, the GENERALLY accepted place to type it is

    A. directly above the address
    B. in the area below where the stamp will be affixed
    C. in the lower left-hand corner
    D. in the upper left-hand corner

24. When taking a citation of a case in shorthand, which of the following should you write FIRST if you are having difficulty keeping up with the dictation?

    A. Volume and page number B. Title of volume
    C. Name of plaintiff   D. Name of defendant

25. All of the following abbreviations and their meanings are correctly paired EXCEPT

    A. viz. - namely   B. ibid. - refer
    C. n.b. - note well   D. q.v. - which see

KEY (CORRECT ANSWERS)

1. D
2. D
3. B
4. B
5. A

6. C
7. D
8. A
9. A
10. C

11. D
12. A
13. B
14. D
15. C

16. B
17. A
18. D
19. C
20. A

21. B
22. B
23. B
24. A
25. B

EXAMINATION SECTION
TEST 1

DIRECTIONS: Each question or incomplete statement is followed by several suggested answers or completions. Select the one that BEST answers the question or completes the statement. *PRINT THE LETTER OF THE CORRECT ANSWER IN THE SPACE AT THE RIGHT.*

Questions 1-9.

DIRECTIONS: Questions 1 through 9 consist of sentences which may or may not be examples of good English usage. Consider grammar, punctuation, spelling, capitalization, awkwardness, etc. Examine each sentence, and then choose the correct statement about it from the four choices below it. If the English usage in the sentence given is better than it would be with any of the changes suggested in options B, C, and D, choose option A. Do not choose an option that will change the meaning of the sentence.

1. According to Judge Frank, the grocer's sons found guilty of assault and sentenced last Thursday.

    A. This is an example of acceptable writing.
    B. A comma should be placed after the word *sentenced*.
    C. The word *were* should be placed after *sons*
    D. The apostrophe in *grocer's* should be placed after the *s*.

2. The department heads assistant said that the stenographers should type duplicate copies of all contracts, leases, and bills.

    A. This is an example of acceptable writing.
    B. A comma should be placed before the word *contracts*.
    C. An apostrophe should be placed before the *s* in *heads*.
    D. Quotation marks should be placed before *the stenographers* and after *bills*.

3. The lawyers questioned the men to determine who was the true property owner?

    A. This is an example of acceptable writing.
    B. The phrase *questioned the men* should be changed to *asked the men questions*.
    C. The word *was* should be changed to *were*.
    D. The question mark should be changed to a period.

4. The terms stated in the present contract are more specific than those stated in the previous contract.

    A. This is an example of acceptable writing.
    B. The word *are* should be changed to *is*.
    C. The word *than* should be changed to *then*.
    D. The word *specific* should be changed to *specified*.

5. Of the lawyers considered, the one who argued more skillful was chosen for the job.

    A. This is an example of acceptable writing.
    B. The word *more* should be replaced by the word *most*.
    C. The word *skillful* should be replaced by the word *skillfully,*
    D. The word *chosen* should be replaced by the word *selected*.

77

6. Each of the states has a court of appeals; some states have circuit courts.   6.____

   A. This is an example of acceptable writing.
   B. The semi-colon should be changed to a comma.
   C. The word *has* should be changed to *have*.
   D. The word *some* should be capitalized.

7. The court trial has greatly effected the child's mental condition.   7.____

   A. This is an example of acceptable writing.
   B. The word *effected* should be changed to *affected*.
   C. The word *greatly* should be placed after *effected*.
   D. The apostrophe in *child's* should be placed after the *s*.

8. Last week, the petition signed by all the officers was sent to the Better Business Bureau.   8.____

   A. This is an example of acceptable writing.
   B. The phrase *last week* should be placed after *officers*.
   C. A comma should be placed after *petition*.
   D. The word *was* should be changed to *were*.

9. Mr. Farrell claims that he requested form A-12, and three booklets describing court procedures.   9.____

   A. This is an example of acceptable writing.
   B. The word *that* should be eliminated.
   C. A colon should be placed after *requested*.
   D. The comma after *A-12* should be eliminated.

Questions 10-21.

DIRECTIONS: Questions 10 through 21 contain a word in capital letters followed by four suggested meanings of the word. For each question, choose the BEST meaning for the word in capital letters.

10. SIGNATORY - A   10.____

    A. lawyer who draws up a legal document
    B. document that must be signed by a judge
    C. person who signs a document
    D. true copy of a signature

11. RETAINER - A   11.____

    A. fee paid to a lawyer for his services
    B. document held by a third party
    C. court decision to send a prisoner back to custody pending trial
    D. legal requirement to keep certain types of files

12. BEQUEATH - To   12.____

    A. receive assistance from a charitable organization
    B. give personal property by will to another
    C. transfer real property from one person to another
    D. receive an inheritance upon the death of a relative

13. RATIFY - To

    A. approve and sanction
    B. forego
    C. produce evidence
    D. summarize

14. CODICIL - A

    A. document introduced in evidence in a civil action
    B. subsection of a law
    C. type of legal action that can be brought by a plaintiff
    D. supplement or an addition to a will

15. ALIAS

    A. Assumed name
    B. In favor of
    C. Against
    D. A writ

16. PROXY - A(n)

    A. phony document in a real estate transaction
    B. opinion by a judge of a civil court
    C. document containing appointment of an agent
    D. summons in a lawsuit

17. ALLEGED

    A. Innocent
    B. Asserted
    C. Guilty
    D. Called upon

18. EXECUTE - To

    A. complete a legal document by signing it
    B. set requirements
    C. render services to a duly elected executive of a municipality
    D. initiate legal action such as a lawsuit

19. NOTARY PUBLIC - A

    A. lawyer who is running for public office
    B. judge who hears minor cases
    C. public officer, one of whose functions is to administer oaths
    D. lawyer who gives free legal services to persons unable to pay

20. WAIVE - To

    A. disturb a calm state of affairs
    B. knowingly renounce a right or claim
    C. pardon someone for a minor fault
    D. purposely mislead a person during an investigation

21. ARRAIGN - To

    A. prevent an escape
    B. defend a prisoner
    C. verify a document
    D. accuse in a court of law

Questions 22-40.

DIRECTIONS: Questions 22 through 40 each consist of four words which may or may not be spelled correctly. If you find an error in
only one word, mark your answer A;
any two words, mark your answer B;
any three words, mark your answer C;
none of these words, mark your answer D.

22.	occurrence	Febuary	privilege	similiar	22.____
23.	separate	transferring	analyze	column	23.____
24.	develop	license	bankrupcy	abreviate	24.____
25.	subpoena	arguement	dissolution	foreclosure	25.____
26.	exaggerate	fundamental	significance	warrant	26.____
27.	citizen	endorsed	marraige	appraissal	27.____
28.	precedant	univercity	observence	preliminary	28.____
29.	stipulate	negligence	judgment	prominent	29.____
30.	judisial	whereas	release	guardian	30.____
31.	appeal	larcenny	transcrip	jurist	31.____
32.	petition	tenancy	agenda	insurance	32.____
33.	superfical	premise	morgaged	maintainance	33.____
34.	testamony	publically	installment	possessed	34.____
35.	escrow	decree	eviction	miscelaneous	35.____
36.	securitys	abeyance	adhere	corporate	36.____
37.	kaleidoscope	anesthesia	vermilion	tafetta	37.____
38.	congruant	barrenness	plebescite	vigilance	38.____
39.	picnicing	promisory	resevoir	omission	39.____
40.	supersede	banister	wholly	seize	40.____

KEY (CORRECT ANSWERS)

1. C	11. A	21. D	31. B
2. C	12. B	22. B	32. D
3. D	13. A	23. D	33. C
4. A	14. D	24. B	34. B
5. C	15. A	25. A	35. A
6. A	16. C	26. D	36. A
7. B	17. B	27. B	37. A
8. A	18. A	28. C	38. B
9. D	19. C	29. D	39. C
10. C	20. B	30. A	40. D

READING COMPREHENSION
UNDERSTANDING AND INTERPRETING WRITTEN MATERIAL
EXAMINATION SECTION
TEST 1

DIRECTIONS: Each question or incomplete statement is followed by several suggested answers or completions. Select the one that BEST answers the question or completes the statement. *PRINT THE LETTER OF THE CORRECT ANSWER IN THE SPACE AT THE RIGHT.*

Questions 1-4.

DIRECTIONS: Questions 1 through 4 are to be answered SOLELY on the basis of the following passage.

Those engaged in the exercise of First Amendment rights by pickets, marches, parades, and open-air assemblies are not exempted from obeying valid local traffic ordinances. In a recent pronouncement, Mr. Justice Baxter, speaking for the Supreme Court, wrote:

The rights of free speech and assembly, while fundamental to our democratic society, still do not mean that everyone with opinions or beliefs to express may address a group at any public place and at any time. The constitutional guarantee of liberty implies the existence of an organized society maintaining public order, without which liberty itself would be lost in the excesses of anarchy. The control of travel on the streets is a clear example of governmental responsibility to insure this necessary order. A restriction in that relation, designed to promote the public convenience in the interest of all, and not susceptible to abuses of discriminatory application, cannot be disregarded by the attempted exercise of some civil rights which, in other circumstances, would be entitled to protection. One would not be justified in ignoring the familiar red light because this was thought to be a means of social protest. Governmental authorities have the duty and responsibility to keep their streets open and available for movement. A group of demonstrators could not insist upon the right to cordon off a street, or entrance to a public or private building, and allow no one to pass who did not agree to listen to their exhortations.

1. Which of the following statements BEST reflects Mr. Justice Baxter's view of the relationship between liberty and public order?

    A. Public order cannot exist without liberty.
    B. Liberty cannot exist without public order.
    C. The existence of liberty undermines the existence of public order.
    D. The maintenance of public order insures the existence of liberty.

1.____

2. According to the above passage, local traffic ordinances result from

    A. governmental limitations on individual liberty
    B. governmental responsibility to insure public order
    C. majority rule as determined by democratic procedures
    D. restrictions on expression of dissent

2.____

3. The above passage suggests that government would be acting improperly if a local traffic ordinance

   A. was enforced in a discriminatory manner
   B. resulted in public inconvenience
   C. violated the right of free speech and assembly
   D. was not essential to public order

4. Of the following, the MOST appropriate title for the above passage is

   A. THE RIGHTS OF FREE SPEECH AND ASSEMBLY
   B. ENFORCEMENT OF LOCAL TRAFFIC ORDINANCES
   C. FIRST AMENDMENT RIGHTS AND LOCAL TRAFFIC ORDINANCES
   D. LIBERTY AND ANARCHY

Questions 5-8

DIRECTIONS: Questions 5 through 8 are to be answered SOLELY on the basis of the following passage

On November 8, 1976, the Supreme Court refused to block the payment of Medicaid funds for elective abortions. The Court's action means that a new Federal statute that bars the use of Federal funds for abortions unless abortion is necessary to save the life of the mother will not go into effect for many months, if at all.

A Federal District Court in Brooklyn ruled the following month that the statute was unconstitutional and ordered that Federal reimbursement for the costs of abortions continue on the same basis as reimbursements for the costs of pregnancy and childbirth-related services.

Technically, what the Court did today was to deny a request by Senator Howard Ramsdell and others for a stay blocking enforcement of the District Court order pending appeal. The Court's action was a victory for New York City. The City's Health and Hospitals Corporation initiated one of the two lawsuits challenging the new statute that led to the District Court's decision. The Corporation also opposed the request for a Supreme Court stay of that decision, telling the Court in a memorandum that a stay would subject the Corporation to a *grave and irreparable injury.*

5. According to the above passage, it would be CORRECT to state that the Health and Hospitals Corporation

   A. joined Senator Ramsdell in his request for a stay
   B. opposed the statute which limited reimbursement for the cost of abortions
   C. claimed that it would experience a loss if the District Court order was enforced
   D. appealed the District Court decision

6. The above passage indicates that the Supreme Court acted in DIRECT response to

   A. a lawsuit initiated by the Health and Hospitals Corporation
   B. a ruling by a Federal District Court
   C. a request for a stay
   D. the passage of a new Federal statute

7. According to the above passage, it would be CORRECT to state that the Supreme Court

    A. blocked enforcement of the District Court order
    B. refused a request for a stay to block enforcement of the Federal statute
    C. ruled that the new Federal statute was unconstitutional
    D. permitted payment of Federal funds for abortion to continue

8. Following are three statements concerning abortion that might be correct:
    I. Abortion costs are no longer to be Federally reimbursed on the same basis as those for pregnancy and childbirth
    II. Federal funds have not been available for abortions except to save the life of the mother
    III. Medicaid has paid for elective abortions in the past

    According to the passage above, which of the following CORRECTLY classifies the above statements into those that are true and those that are not true?

    A. I is true, but II and III are not.
    B. I and III are true, but II is not.
    C. I and II are true, but III is not.
    D. III is true, but I and II are not.

Questions 9-12.

DIRECTIONS: Questions 9 through 12 are to be answered SOLELY on the basis of the following passage.

A person may use physical force upon another person when and to the extent he reasonably believes such to be necessary to defend himself or a third person from what he reasonably believes to be the use or imminent use of unlawful physical force by such other person, unless (a) the latter's conduct was provoked by the actor himself with intent to cause physical injury to another person; or (b) the actor was the initial aggressor; or (c) the physical force involved is the product of a combat by agreement not specifically authorized by law.

A person may not use deadly physical force upon another person under the circumstances specified above unless (a) he reasonably believes that such other person is using or is about to use deadly physical force. Even in such case, however, the actor may not use deadly physical force if he knows he can, with complete safety, as to himself and others avoid the necessity of doing so by retreating; except that he is under no duty to retreat if he is in his dwelling and is not the initial aggressor; or (b) he reasonably believes that such other person is committing or attempting to commit a kidnapping, forcible rape, or forcible sodomy.

9. Jones and Smith, who have not met before, get into an argument in a tavern. Smith takes a punch at Jones, but misses. Jones then hits Smith on the chin with his fist. Smith falls to the floor and suffers minor injuries.
    According to the above passage, it would be CORRECT to state that _____ justified in using physical force.

    A. only Smith was
    B. only Jones was
    C. both Smith and Jones were
    D. neither Smith nor Jones was

10. While walking down the street, Brady observes Miller striking Mrs. Adams on the head with his fist in an attempt to steal her purse.
According to the above passage, it would be CORRECT to state that Brady would

   A. not be justified in using deadly physical force against Miller since Brady can safely retreat
   B. be justified in using physical force against Miller but not deadly physical force
   C. not be justified in using physical force against Miller since Brady himself is not being attacked
   D. be justified in using deadly physical force

11. Winters is attacked from behind by Sharp, who attempts to beat up Winters with a blackjack. Winters disarms Sharp and succeeds in subduing him with a series of blows to the head. Sharp stops fighting and explains that he thought Winters was the person who had robbed his apartment a few minutes before, but now realizes his mistake.
According to the above passage, it would be CORRECT to state that

   A. Winters was justified in using physical force on Sharp only to the extent necessary to defend himself
   B. Winters was not justified in using physical force on Sharp since Sharp's attack was provoked by what he believed to be Winters' behavior
   C. Sharp was justified in using physical force on Winters since he reasonably believed that Winters had unlawfully robbed him
   D. Winters was justified in using physical force on Sharp only because Sharp was acting mistakenly in attacking him

12. Roberts hears a noise in the cellar of his home, and, upon investigation, discovers an intruder, Welch. Welch moves towards Roberts in a threatening manner, thrusts his hand into a bulging pocket, and withdraws what appears to be a gun. Roberts thereupon strikes Welch over the head with a golf club. He then sees that the *gun* is a toy. Welch later dies of head injuries. According to the above passage, it would be CORRECT to state that Roberts was

   A. justified in using deadly physical force because he reasonably believed Welch was about to use deadly physical force
   B. not justified in using deadly physical force
   C. justified in using deadly physical force only because he did not provoke Welch's conduct
   D. justified in using deadly physical force only because he was not the initial aggressor

Questions 13-16.

DIRECTIONS: Questions 13 through 16 are to be answered SOLELY on the basis of the following passage.

From the beginning, the Supreme Court has supervised the fairness of trials conducted by the Federal government. But the Constitution, as originally drafted, gave the court no such general authority in state cases. The court's power to deal with state cases comes from the Fourteenth Amendment, which became part of the Constitution in 1868. The crucial provision forbids any state to *deprive any person of life, liberty, or property without due process of law.*

The guarantee of *due process* would seem, at the least, to require fair procedure in criminal trials. But curiously the Supreme Court did not speak on the question for many decades. During that time, however, the due process clause was interpreted to bar *unreasonable* state economic regulations, such as minimum wage laws.

In 1915, there came the case of Leo M. Frank, a Georgian convicted of murder in a trial that he contended was dominated by mob hysteria. Historians now agree that there was such hysteria, with overtones of anti-semitism.

The Supreme Court held that it could not look past the findings of the Georgia courts that there had been no mob atmosphere at the trial. Justices Oliver Wendell Holmes and Charles Evans Hughes dissented, arguing that the constitutional guarantee would be *a barren one* if the Federal courts could not make their own inferences from the facts.

In 1923, the case of Moore v. Dempsey involved five Arkansas Blacks convicted of murder and sentenced to death in a community so aroused against them that at one point they were saved from lynching only by Federal troops. Witnesses against them were said to have been beaten into testifying.

The court, though not actually setting aside the convictions, directed a lower Federal court to hold a habeas corpus hearing to find out whether the trial had been fair, or whether the whole proceeding had been *a mask—that counsel, jury, and judge were swept to the fatal end by an irresistible wave of public passion.*

13. According to the above passage, the Supreme Court's INITIAL interpretation of the Fourteenth Amendment

    A. protected state supremacy in economic matters
    B. increased the scope of Federal jurisdiction
    C. required fair procedures in criminal trials
    D. prohibited the enactment of minimum wage laws

14. According to the above passage, the Supreme Court in the Frank case

    A. denied that there had been mob hysteria at the trial
    B. decided that the guilty verdict was supported by the evidence
    C. declined to question the state court's determination of the facts
    D. found that Leo Frank had not received *due process*

15. According to the above passage, the dissenting judges in the Frank case maintained that

    A. due process was an empty promise in the circumstances of that case
    B. the Federal courts could not guarantee certain provisions of the Constitution
    C. the Federal courts should not make their own inferences from the facts in state cases
    D. the Supreme Court had rendered the Constitution *barren*

16. Of the following, the MOST appropriate title for the above passage is
    A. THE CONDUCT OF FEDERAL TRIALS
    B. THE DEVELOPMENT OF STATES' RIGHTS: 1868-1923
    C. MOORE V. DEMPSEY: A CASE STUDY IN CRIMINAL JUSTICE
    D. DUE PROCESS-THE EVOLUTION OF A CONSTITUTIONAL CORNERSTONE

Questions 17-20.

DIRECTIONS: Questions 17 through 20 are to be answered SOLELY on the basis of the following passage.

The difficulty experienced in determining which party has the burden of proving payment or non-payment is due largely to a lack of consistency between the rules of pleading and the rules of proof. In some cases, a plaintiff is obligated by a rule of pleading to allege non-payment on his complaint, yet is not obligated to prove non-payment on the trial. An action upon a contract for the payment of money will serve as an illustration. In such a case, the plaintiff must allege non-payment in his complaint, but the burden of proving payment on the trial is upon the defendant. An important and frequently cited case on this problem is Conkling v. Weatherwax. In that case, the action was brought to establish and enforce a legacy as a lien upon real property. The defendant alleged in her answer that the legacy had been paid. There was no witness competent to testify for the plaintiff to show that the legacy had not been paid. Therefore, the question of the burden of proof became of primary importance since, if the plaintiff had the burden of proving non-payment, she must fail in her action; whereas if the burden of proof was on the defendant to prove payment, the plaintiff might win. The Court of Appeals held that the burden of proof was on the plaintiff. In the course of his opinion, Judge Vann attempted to harmonize the conflicting cases on this subject, and for that purpose formulated three rules. These rules have been construed and applied to numerous subsequent cases. As so construed and applied, these may be summarized as follows:

Rule 1. In an action upon a contract for the payment of money only, where the complaint does not allege a balance due over and above all payments made, the plaintiff must allege nonpayment in his complaint, but the burden of proving payment is upon the defendant. In such a case, payment is an affirmative defense which the defendant must plead in his answer. If the defendant fails to plead payment, but pleads a general denial instead, he will not be permitted to introduce evidence of payment.

Rule 2. Where the complaint sets forth a balance in excess of all payments, owing to the structure of the pleading, burden is upon the plaintiff to prove his allegation. In this case, the defendant is not required to plead payment as a defense in his answer but may introduce evidence of payment under a general denial.

Rule 3. When the action is not upon contract for the payment of money, but is upon an obligation created by operation of law, or is for the enforcement of a lien where non-payment of the amount secured is part of the cause of action, it is necessary both to allege and prove the fact of nonpayment.

17. In the above passage, the case of Conkling v. Weatherwax was cited PRIMARILY to illustrate

    A. a case where the burden of proof was on the defendant to prove payment
    B. how the question of the burden of proof can affect the outcome of a case
    C. the effect of a legacy as a lien upon real property
    D. how conflicting cases concerning the burden of proof were harmonized

18. According to the above passage, the pleading of payment is a defense in Rule(s)

    A. 1, but not Rules 2 and 3
    B. 2, but not Rules 1 and 3
    C. 1 and 3, but not Rule 2
    D. 2 and 3, but not Rule 1

19. The facts in Conkling v. Weatherwax CLOSELY resemble the conditions described in

    A. Rule #1
    B. Rule #2
    C. Rule #3
    D. none of the rules

20. The MAJOR topic of the above passage may BEST be described as

    A. determining the ownership of property
    B. providing a legal definition
    C. placing the burden of proof
    D. formulating rules for deciding cases

Questions 21-25.

DIRECTIONS: Questions 21 through 25 are to be answered SOLELY on the basis of the following passage.

The law is quite clear that evidence obtained in violation of Section 605 of the Federal Communications Act is not admissible in Federal court. However, the law as to the admissibility of evidence in state court is far from clear. Had the Supreme Court of the United States made the wiretap exclusionary rule applicable to the states, such confusion would not exist.

In the case of Alton v. Texas, the Supreme Court was called upon to determine whether wiretapping by state and local officers came within the proscription of the Federal statute and, if so, whether Section 605 required the same remedies for its vindication in state courts. In answer to the first question, Mr. Justice Minton, speaking for the court, flatly stated that Section 605 made it a federal crime for anyone to intercept telephone messages and divulge what he learned. The court went on to say that a state officer who testified in state court concerning the existence, contents, substance, purport, effect, or meaning of an intercepted conversation violated the Federal law and committed a criminal act. In regard to the second question, how-ever, the Supreme Court felt constrained by due regard for federal-state relations to answer in the negative. Mr. Justice Minton stated that the court would not presume, in the absence of a clear manifestation of congressional intent, that Congress intended to supersede state rules of evidence.

Because the Supreme Court refused to apply the exclusionary rule to wiretap evidence that was being used in state courts, the states respectively made this decision for themselves. According to hearings held before a congressional committee in 1975, six states authorize wiretapping by statute, 33 states impose total bans on wiretapping, and 11 states have no definite statute on the subject. For examples of extremes, a statute in Pennsylvania will be compared with a statute in New York.

The Pennsylvania statute provides that no communications by telephone or telegraph can be intercepted without permission of both parties. It also specifically prohibits such interception by public officials and provides that evidence obtained cannot be used in court.

The lawmakers in New York, recognizing the need for legal wire-tapping, authorized wiretapping by statute. A New York law authorizes the issuance of an ex parte order upon oath or affirmation for limited wiretapping. The aim of the New York law is to allow court-ordered wiretapping and to encourage the testimony of state officers concerning such wiretapping in court. The New York law was found to be constitutional by the New York State Supreme Court in 1975. Other states, including Oregon, Maryland, Nevada, and Massachusetts, enacted similar laws which authorize court-ordered wiretapping.

To add to this legal disarray, the vast majority of the states, including New Jersey and New York, permit wiretapping evidence to be received in court even though obtained in violation of the state laws and of Section 605 of the Federal act. However, some states, such as Rhode Island, have enacted statutory exclusionary rules which provide that illegally procured wiretap evidence is incompetent in civil as well as criminal actions.

21. According to the above passage, a state officer who testifies in New York State court concerning the contents of a conversation he overheard through a court-ordered wire-tap is in violation of _____ law.

    A. state law but not federal
    B. federal law but not state
    C. federal law and state
    D. neither federal nor state

22. According to the above passage, which of the following statements concerning states statutes on wiretapping is CORRECT?

    A. The number of states that impose total bans on wiretapping is three times as great as the number of states with no definite statute on wiretapping.
    B. The number of states having no definite statute on wiretapping is more than twice the number of states authorizing wiretapping.
    C. The number of states which authorize wiretapping by statute and the number of states having no definite statute on wiretapping exceed the number of states imposing total bans on wiretapping.
    D. More states authorize wiretapping by statute than impose total bans on wiretapping.

23. Following are three statements concerning wiretapping that might be valid:

   I. In Pennsylvania, only public officials may legally intercept telephone communications.
   II. In Rhode Island, evidence obtained through an illegal wiretap is incompetent in criminal, but not civil, actions.
   III. Neither Massachusetts nor Pennsylvania authorizes wiretapping by public officials.

   According to the above passage, which of the following CORRECTLY classifies these statements into those that are valid and those that are not?

   A. I is valid, but II and III are not.
   B. II is valid, but I and III are not.
   C. II and III are valid, but I is not.
   D. None of the statements is valid.

24. According to the above passage, evidence obtained in violation of Section 605 of the Federal Communications Act is inadmissible in

   A. federal court but not in any state courts
   B. federal court and all state courts
   C. all state courts but not in federal court
   D. federal court and some state courts

25. In regard to state rules of evidence, Mr. Justice Minton expressed the Court's opinion that Congress

   A. intended to supersede state rules of evidence, as manifested by Section 605 of the Federal Communications Act
   B. assumed that federal statutes would govern state rules of evidence in all wiretap cases
   C. left unclear whether it intended to supersede state rules of evidence
   D. precluded itself from superseding state rules of evidence through its regard for federal-state relations

KEY (CORRECT ANSWERS)

1.	B	11.	A
2.	B	12.	A
3.	A	13.	D
4.	C	14.	C
5.	B	15.	A
6.	C	16.	D
7.	D	17.	B
8.	D	18.	A
9.	B	19.	C
10.	B	20.	C

21. B
22. A
23. D
24. D
25. C

TEST 2

DIRECTIONS: Each question or incomplete statement is followed by several suggested answers or completions. Select the one that BEST answers the question or completes the Statement. *PRINT THE LETTER OF THE CORRECT ANSWER IN THE SPACE AT THE RIGHT.*

Questions 1-3.

DIRECTIONS: Questions 1 through 3 are to be answered SOLELY on the basis of the following passage.

    The State Assembly has passed a bill that would require all state agencies, public authorities, and local governments to refuse bids in excess of $2,000 from any foreign firm or corporation. The only exceptions to this outright prohibition against public buying of foreign goods or services would be for products not available in this country, goods of a quality unobtainable from an American supplier, and products using foreign materials that are *substantially* manufactured in the United States.

    This bill is a flagrant violation of the United States' officially espoused trade principles. It would add to the costs of state and local governments. It could provoke retaliatory action from many foreign governments against the state and other American producers, and foreign governments would be fully entitled to take such retaliatory action under the General Agreement on Tariffs and Trade, which the United States has signed.

    The State Senate, which now has the Assembly bill before it, should reject this protectionist legislation out of enlightened regard for the interests of the taxpayers and producers of the State—as well as for those of the nation and its trading partners generally. In this time of unemployment and international monetary disorder, the State—with its reputation for intelligent and progressive law-making—should avoid contributing to what could become a tidal wave of protectionism here and overseas.

1. Under the requirements of the bill passed by the State Assembly, a bid from a foreign manufacturer in excess of $2,000 can be accepted by a state agency or local government only if it meets which one of the following requirements?
The

   A. bid is approved individually by the State Legislature
   B. bidder is willing to accept payment in United States currency
   C. bid is for an item of a quality unobtainable from an American supplier
   D. bid is for an item which would be more expensive if it were purchased from an American supplier

2. The author of the above passage feels that the bill passed by the State Assembly should be

   A. passed by the State Senate and put into effect
   B. passed by the State Senate but vetoed by the Governor
   C. reintroduced into the State Assembly and rejected
   D. rejected by the State Senate

3. The author of the above passage calls the practice of prohibiting purchase of products manufactured by foreign countries

   A. prohibition
   B. protectionism
   C. retaliatory action
   D. isolationism

Questions 4-7.

DIRECTIONS: Questions 4 through 7 are to be answered SOLELY on the basis of the following passage.

   Data processing is by no means a new invention. In one form or another, it has been carried on throughout the entire history of civilization. In its most general sense, data processing means organizing data so that it can be used for a specific purpose-a procedure commonly known simply as *record-keeping* or *paperwork*. With the development of modern office equipment, and particularly with the recent introduction of computers, the techniques of data processing have become highly elaborate and sophisticated, but the basic purpose remains the same: Turning raw data into useful information.

   The key concept here is usefulness. The data, or input, that is to be processed can be compared to the raw material that is to go into a manufacturing process. The information, or output, that results from data processing—like the finished product of a manufacturer—should be clearly usable. A collection of data has little value unless it is converted into information that serves a specific function.

4. The expression *paperwork,* as it is used in this passage,

   A. shows that the author regards such operations as a waste of time
   B. has the same general meaning as *data processing*
   C. refers to methods of record-keeping that are no longer in use
   D. indicates that the public does not understand the purpose of data processing

5. The above passage indicates that the use of computers has

   A. greatly simplified the clerical work in an office
   B. led to more complicated systems for the handling of data
   C. had no effect whatsoever on data processing
   D. made other modern office machines obsolete

6. Which of the following BEST expresses the basic principle of data processing as it is described in the above passage?

   A. Input-processing-output
   B. Historical record-keeping-modern techniques -specific functions
   C. Office equipment-computer-accurate data
   D. Raw material-manufacturer-retailer

7. According to the above passage, data processing may be described as

   A. a new management technique
   B. computer technology
   C. information output
   D. record-keeping

Questions 8-10.

DIRECTIONS: Questions 8 through 10 are to be answered SOLELY on the basis of the following passage.

A loan receipt is an instrument devised to permit the insurance company to bring an action against the wrongdoer in the name of the insured despite the fact that the insured no longer has any financial interest in the outcome. It provides, in effect, that the amount of the loss is advanced to the insured as a loan which is repayable only up to the extent of any recovery made from the wrongdoer. The insured further agrees to enter and prosecute suit against the wrongdoer in his own name. Such a receipt substitutes a loan for a payment for the purpose of permitting the insurance company to press its action against the wrongdoer in the name of the insured.

8. According to the above passage, the purpose behind the use of a loan receipt is to 8.____

   A. guarantee that the insurance company gets repayment from the person insured
   B. insure repayment of all expenditures to the named insured
   C. make it possible for the insurance company to sue in the name of the policyowner
   D. prevent the wrongdoer from escaping the natural consequences of his act

9. According to the above passage, the amount of the loan which must be paid back to the insurance company equals but does NOT exceed the amount 9.____

   A. of the loss
   B. on the face of the policy
   C. paid to the insured
   D. recovered from the wrongdoer

10. According to the above passage, by giving a loan receipt, the person insured agrees to 10.____

    A. a suit against the wrongdoer in his own name
    B. forego any financial gain from the outcome of the suit
    C. institute an action on behalf of the insurance company
    D. repay the insurance company for the loan received

Questions 11-12.

DIRECTIONS: Questions 11 and 12 are to be answered SOLELY on the basis of the following passage.

Open air markets originally came into existence spontaneously when groups of pushcart peddlers congregated in spots where business was good. Good business induced them to return to these spots daily and, thus, unofficial open air markets arose. These peddlers paid no fees, and the city received no revenue from them. Confusion and disorder reigned in these unsupervised markets; the earliest arrivals secured the best locations, unless or until forcibly ejected by stronger or tougher peddlers. Although the open air markets supplied a definite need in the community, there were many detrimental factors involved in their operation. They were unsightly, created unsanitary conditions in market streets by the deposit of garbage and waste and were a definite obstruction to traffic, as well as a fire hazard.

11. On the basis of the above passage, the MOST accurate of the following statements is:

   A. Each peddler in the original open air markets had his own fixed location.
   B. Open air markets were originally organized by means of agreements between groups of pushcart peddlers.
   C. The locations of these markets depended upon the amount of business the vendors were able to do.
   D. There was confusion and disorder in these open air markets because the peddlers were not required to pay any fees to the city.

12. Of the following, the MOST valid implication which can be made on the basis of the above passage is that the

   A. detrimental aspect of the operations of open air markets was the probable reason for the creation of enclosed markets under the supervision of the Department of Markets
   B. open air markets could not supply any community need without proper supervision
   C. original open air markets were good examples of the operation of fair competition in business
   D. possibility of obtaining a source of revenue was probably the most important reason for the city's ultimate undertaking of the supervision of open air markets

Questions 13-14.

DIRECTIONS: Questions 13 and 14 are to be answered SOLELY on the basis of the following passage.

   A person who displays on his window, door, or in his place of business words or letters in Hebraic characters other than the word *kosher,* or any sign, emblem, insignia, six-pointed star, symbol or mark in simulation of same, without displaying in conjunction there-with in English letters of at least the same size as such characters, signs, emblems, insignia or marks, the words *we sell kosher meat and food only* or *we sell non-kosher meat and food only* or *we sell both kosher and non-kosher meat and food,* as the case may be, is guilty of a misdemeanor. Possession of non-kosher meat and food in any place of business advertising the sale of kosher meat and food only is presumptive evidence that the person in possession exposes the same for sale with intent to defraud, in violation of the provisions of this section.

13. Of the following, the MOST valid implication that can be made on the basis of the above passage is that a person who

   A. displays on his window a six-pointed star in addition to the word *kosher* in Hebraic letters is guilty of intent to defraud
   B. displays on his window the word *kosher* in Hebraic characters intends to indicate that he has only kosher food for sale
   C. sells both kosher and non-kosher food in the same place of business is guilty of a misdemeanor
   D. sells only that type of food which can be characterized as neither kosher nor non-kosher, such as fruit and vegetables, without an explanatory sign in English is guilty of intent to defraud

14. Of the following, the one which would constitute a violation of the rules of the above passage is a case in which a person

    A. displays the word *kosher* on his window in Hebraic letters has only kosher meat and food in the store but has some non-kosher meat in the rear of the establishment
    B. selling both kosher and non-kosher meat and food uses words in Hebraic letters, other than the word *kosher,* on his window and a sign of the same size letters in English stating *we sell both kosher and non-kosher meat and food*
    C. selling only kosher meat and food uses words in Hebraic letters, other than the word *kosher,* on his window and a sign of the same size letters in English stating *we sell kosher meat and food only*
    D. selling only non-kosher meat and food displays a six-pointed star on his window and a sign of the same size letters in English stating *we sell only non-kosher meat and food*

Questions 15-16.

DIRECTIONS: Questions 15 and 16 are to be answered SOLELY on the basis of the following passage.

COMMODITIES IN GLASS BOTTLES OR JARS

The contents of the bottle may be stated in terms of weight or of fluid measure, the weight being indicated in terms of pounds and ounces and the fluid measure being indicated in terms of gallons, quarts, pints, half-pints, gills, or fluid ounces. When contents are liquid, the amount should not be stated in terms of weight. The marking indicating content is to be on a tag attached to the bottle or upon a label. The letters shall be in bold-faced type at least one-ninth of an inch (1/9") in height for bottles or jars having a capacity of a gill, half-pint, pint, or multiples of a pint, and letters at least three-sixteenths of an inch (3/16") in height for bottles of other capacities, on a part of the tag or label free from other printing or ornamentation, leaving a clear space around the marking which indicates the contents.

15. Of the following, the one which does NOT meet the requirements of the above passage is a

    A. bottle of cooking oil with a label stating *contents—16 fluid ounces* in appropriate sized letters
    B. bottle of vinegar with a label stating *contents—8 ounces avoir.* in appropriate sized letters
    C. glass jar filled with instant coffee with a label stating *contents—1 lb. 3 ozs. avoir.* in appropriate sized letters
    D. glass jar filled with liquid bleach with a label stating *contents—1 quart* in appropriate sized letters

16. Of the following, the one which does meet the requirements of the above passage is a

    A. bottle filled with a low-calorie liquid sweetener with a label stating *contents—3 fluid ounces* in letters 1/12" high
    B. bottle filled with ammonia solution for cleaning with a label stating *contents—1 pint* in letters 1/10" high

C. jar filled with baking powder with a label stating *contents—$\frac{1}{2}$ pint* in letters $\frac{1}{4}$" high

D. jar filled with hard candy with a label stating *contents—1 lb. avoir.* in letters $\frac{1}{2}$" high

Question 17.

DIRECTIONS: Question 17 is to be answered SOLELY on the basis of the information contained in the following passage.

DEALERS IN SECOND HAND DEVICES

1. It shall be unlawful for any person to engage in or conduct the business of dealing in, trading in, selling, receiving, or repairing condemned, rebuilt, or used weighing or measuring devices without a permit therefor.

2. Such permit shall expire on the twenty-eighth day of February next succeeding the date of issuance thereof.

3. Every person engaged in the above business, within five days after the making of a repair, or the sale and delivery of a repaired, rebuilt, or used weighing or measuring device, shall serve notice in writing on the commissioner giving the name and address of the person for whom the repair has been made or to whom a repaired, rebuilt, or used weighing or measuring device has been sold or delivered, and shall include a statement that such device has been so altered, repaired, or rebuilt as to conform to the regulations of the department.

17. According to the above passage, the MOST accurate of the following statements is: 17.____

   A. A permit issued to engage in the business mentioned above, first issued on April 23, 1968, expired on February 28, 1969.
   B. A rebuilt or repaired weighing or measuring device should not operate with less error than the tolerances permitted by the regulations of the department.
   C. If a used scale in good condition is sold, it is not necessary for the seller to notify the commissioner of the name and address of the buyer.
   D. There is a difference in the time required to notify the commissioner of a repair or of a sale of a repaired device.

Questions 18-19.

DIRECTIONS: Questions 18 and 19 are to be answered SOLELY on the basis of the following passage.

   A. It shall be unlawful for any person, firm, or corporation to sell or offer for sale at retail for use in internal combustion engines in motor vehicles any gasoline unless such seller shall post and keep continuously posted on the individual pump or other dispensing device from which such gasoline is sold or offered for sale a sign or placard not less than seven inches in height and eight inches in width nor larger than twelve inches in height and twelve inches in width and stating clearly in numbers of uniform size the selling price or prices per gallon of such gasoline so sold or offered for sale from such pump or other dispensing device.

B. The amount of governmental tax to be collected in connection with the sale of such gasoline shall be stated on such sign or placard and separately and apart from such selling price or prices.

18. The one of the following price signs posted on a gasoline pump which would be in violation of the above passage is a sign _____ square inches in size and _____ inches high.

    A. 144; 12   B. 84; 7   C. 72; 12   D. 60; 8

19. According to the above passage, the LEAST accurate of the following statements is:

    A. Gasoline may be sold from a dispensing device other than a pump.
    B. If two different pumps are used to sell the same grade of gasoline, a price sign must appear on each pump.
    C. The amount of governmental tax and the price of the gasoline must not be stated on the same sign.
    D. The sizes of the numbers used on a sign to indicate the price of gasoline must be the same.

Questions 20-21.

DIRECTIONS: Questions 20 and 21 are to be answered SOLELY on the basis of the following passage.

In all systems of weights and measures based on one or more arbitrary fundamental units, the concrete representation of the unit in the form of a standard is necessary, and the construction and preservation of such a standard is a matter of primary importance. Therefore, it is essential that the standard should be so constructed as to be as nearly permanent and invariable as human ingenuity can contrive. The reference of all measures to an original standard is essential for their correctness, and such a standard must be maintained and preserved in its integrity by some responsible authority which is thus able to provide against the use of false weights and measures. Accordingly, from earliest times, standards were constructed and preserved under the direction of kings and priests, and the temples were a favorite place for their deposit. Later, this duty was assumed by the government, and today we find the integrity of standards of weights and measures safeguarded by international agreement.

20. Of the following, the MOST valid implication which can be made on the basis of the above passage is that

    A. fundamental units of systems of weights and measures should be represented by quantities so constructed that they are specific and constant
    B. in the earliest times, standards were so constructed that they were as permanent and invariable as modern ones
    C. international agreement has practically relieved the U.S. government of the necessity of preserving standards of weights and measures
    D. the preservation of standards is of less importance than the ingenuity used in their construction

21. Of the following, the MOST appropriate title for the above passage is 21._____
    A. THE CONSTRUCTION AND PRESERVATION OF STANDARDS OF WEIGHTS AND MEASURES
    B. THE FIXING OF RESPONSIBILITY FOR THE ESTABLISHMENT OF STANDARDS OF WEIGHTS AND MEASURES
    C. THE HISTORY OF SYSTEMS OF WEIGHTS AND MEASURES
    D. THE VALUE OF PROPER STANDARDS IN PROVIDING CORRECT WEIGHTS AND MEASURES

Questions 22-23.

DIRECTIONS: Questions 22 and 23 are to be answered SOLELY on the basis of the following passage.

Accurate weighing and good scales insure that excess is not given just for the sake of good measure. No more striking example of the fundamental importance of correct weighing to the business man is found than in the simple and usual relation where a charge or value is obtained by multiplying a weight by a unit price. For example, a scale may weigh *light,* that is, the actual quantity delivered is in excess by 1 percent. The actual result is that the seller taxes himself. If his profit is supposed to be 10 percent of total sales, an overweight of 1 percent represents 10 percent of that profit. Under these conditions, the situation is as though the seller were required to pay a sales tax equivalent to what he is taxing himself.

22. Of the following, the MOST valid implication which can be made on the basis of the above passage is that 22._____

    A. consistent use of scales that weigh *light* will reduce sellers' profits
    B. no good businessman would give any buyer more than the weight required even if his scale is accurate
    C. the kind of situation described in the above passage could not arise if sales were being made of merchandise sold by the yard
    D. the use of incorrect scales is one of the reasons causing governments to impose sales taxes

23. According to the above passage, the MOST accurate of the following statements is: 23._____

    A. If his scale weighs *light* by an amount of 2 percent, the seller would deliver only 98 pounds when 100 pounds was the amount agreed upon.
    B. If the seller's scale weighs *heavy,* the buyer will receive an amount in excess of what he intended to purchase.
    C. If the seller's scale weighs *light* by an amount of 1 percent, a buyer who agreed to purchase 50 pounds of merchandise would actually receive $50 \frac{1}{2}$ pounds.
    D. The use of a scale which delivers an amount which is in excess of that required is an example of deliberate fraud.

Questions 24-25.

DIRECTIONS: Questions 24 and 25 are to be answered SOLELY on the basis of the following passage.

Food shall be deemed to be misbranded:
1. If its labeling is false or misleading in any particular.

2. If any word, statement, or other information required by or under authority of this article to appear on the label or labeling is not prominently placed thereon with such conspicuousness (as compared with other words, statements, designs, or devices in the labeling) and in such terms as to render it likely to be read and understood by the ordinary individual under customary conditions of purchase and use.

3. If it purports to be or is represented as a food for which a standard of quality has been prescribed and its quality falls below such standard, unless its label bears a statement that it falls below such standard.

24. According to the above passage, the MOST accurate of the following statements is:

    A. A food may be considered misbranded if the label contains a considerable amount of information which is not required.
    B. If a consumer purchased one type of canned food, although he intended to buy another, the food is probably misbranded.
    C. If a food is used in large amounts by a group of people of certain foreign origin, it can be considered misbranded unless the label is in the foreign language with which they are familiar.
    D. The required information on a label is likely to be in larger print than other information which may appear on it.

25. According to the above passage, the one of the following foods which may be considered to be misbranded is a

    A. can of peaches with a label which carries the brand name of the packer but states *Below Standard in Quality*
    B. can of vegetables with a label on which is printed a shield which states *U.S. Grade B*
    C. package of frozen food which has some pertinent information printed on it in very small type which a customer cannot read and which the store manager cannot read when asked to do so by the customer
    D. package of margarine of the same size as the usual package of butter, kept near the butter, but clearly labeled as margarine

KEY (CORRECT ANSWERS)

1. C
2. D
3. B
4. B
5. B

6. A
7. D
8. C
9. D
10. A

11. C
12. A
13. B
14. A
15. B

16. D
17. A
18. C
19. C
20. A

21. D
22. A
23. C
24. D
25. C

EXAMINATION SECTION
TEST 1

DIRECTIONS: Each question or incomplete statement is followed by several suggested answers or completions. Select the one that BEST answers the question or completes the statement. *PRINT THE LETTER OF THE CORRECT ANSWER IN THE SPACE AT THE RIGHT.*

1. Assume that as supervisor of a central transcribing unit you are considering the establishment of a new procedure to check the accuracy of your subordinates' work. Of the following, the MOST important factor which you should consider before deciding to establish such a procedure is

    A. whether or not your subordinates are likely to resent your use of the new procedure
    B. the frequency with which it will be practicable to check the accuracy of your subordinates' work
    C. the phases of your subordinates' work which will require the greatest amount of review
    D. whether or not the expected results of the new procedure will justify the time and money spent on using it

1.____

2. Suppose that because of a shortage of stenographers, the head of a bureau in a city agency has assigned one stenographer to handle all the stenographic work of two units in the bureau. Whenever the stenographer is given an assignment by the supervisor of either unit, she is told that the assignment is important and that it is to be completed immediately. The stenographer is constantly criticized by one or the other of these supervisors for failing to complete work assignments on time.
This situation may BEST be described as an example of the

    A. failure of a subordinate to determine the order in which tasks should be done
    B. failure of a supervisor to supervise closely the work of a subordinate
    C. inadvisability of having a subordinate work for more than one supervisor at a time
    D. inability of a supervisor to give clear instructions when assigning work to a subordinate

2.____

3. As supervisor of a stenographic unit, you find that an important report prepared and checked for accuracy jointly by two of your stenographers contains a serious, careless mistake. One of the stenographers has a good work record, while the other is known to be a careless worker with a record of low production.
Of the following, the MOST appropriate action for you to take in this matter is to explain to the stenographers the consequences of the mistake and to

    A. urge the more efficient stenographer to be more careful in checking the accuracy of the other stenographer's work
    B. impress the less efficient stenographer with the importance of checking her work thoroughly
    C. make certain that these two stenographers are not assigned to work together in preparing future reports
    D. emphasize to both employees that they must be more careful in their work

3.____

103

4. *The employees of an agency can usually make valuable contributions toward improving the methods and procedures used in the agency.*
   The extent to which the employees of an agency willingly participate in improving methods and procedures is dependent PRIMARILY on the

   A. extent to which employees specialize in performing certain specific duties
   B. encouragement the agency gives to the employees to contribute to methods improvement
   C. amount of time during the workday that employees can devote to planning suggestions
   D. level of difficulty of the work performed by the employees

5. Assume that you have been assigned as the leader of an employee training conference dealing with supervisory techniques and problems. At the sessions of the conference, one of the participants frequently asks you questions, the answers to which would require you to express your own opinion on the problem under discussion.
   Of the following, the LEAST effective method to use in handling such a question is for you to

   A. refer the question to the conference as a whole
   B. request the participant asking the question to give his own opinion
   C. direct the question to a participant who has had experience with such type of problem
   D. answer the question directly with your own opinion and then ask the participants if they concur

6. *It is possible to have accurate work measurement without having satisfactory work standards, but it is not possible to have satisfactory work standards unless they are based upon accurate work measurement.*
   The one of the following statements which is the MOST direct implication of this quotation is that

   A. the number of lines that a typist types must be compared with a satisfactory work standard
   B. satisfactory work standards for the number of lines that a typist is required to type depend upon accurate work measurement
   C. the establishment of satisfactory work standards is necessary before work can be accurately measured
   D. accurate work measurement is of most value when it is used for the development of satisfactory work standards

7. Assume that you are the supervisor of a central stenographic unit that has just been organized in your agency. One of the stenographers who are being transferred to your unit has been reported as uncooperative in working with her former supervisor and as using unauthorized work procedures rather than following procedures prescribed by her supervisor.
   Of the following actions, the MOST appropriate one for you to take FIRST when this stenographer reports to you for work is to

A. explain to her immediately that you cannot permit her to use procedures other than those that you prescribe for use
B. display confidence in her by encouraging her to use her judgment as to methods of performing her work
C. discuss her new assignment with her without referring to her reported uncooperative attitude
D. indicate to her that you are aware of her uncooperative attitude but that, nevertheless, you expect her to cooperate fully with you

8. *The channels of communication between the management of a bureau and its employees not only should be kept open and working but they should also be two-way channels.*
Of the following, the MOST effective method for a supervisor to use to carry out this recommendation is to

   A. arrange periodic staff meetings and individual conferences to discuss problems and procedures with his subordinates
   B. change subordinates' assignments regularly so that they will be able to see how their work is related to the objectives of the bureau
   C. issue regular instructions, both written and oral, which clearly show each subordinate's assignments
   D. encourage his subordinates to discuss personal problems with him

9. *Work measurement is an essential control tool to an office supervisor.*
Of the following, the LEAST important reason for using work measurement as a control tool is that work measurement

   A. may indicate training needs of his subordinates
   B. simplifies the procedures used by the supervisor's subordinates in carrying out their assignments
   C. can indicate whether the supervisor is employing more subordinates than he really needs
   D. is a basis for determining which of the supervisor's subordinates are his most efficient employees

10. *Internal management reporting in government agencies is becoming more statistical in nature. Statistics have thus become a major tool in management supervision in public agencies.*
Before deciding to adopt statistical reporting as a management tool, the management of a public agency should FIRST determine whether the

    A. employees of the agency understand the need for, and the use of, statistics in reporting
    B. supervisory staff in the agency is capable of putting reports into statistical form
    C. major activities of the agency can be reported statistically
    D. present achievements of the agency can be compared statistically with those of previous years

Questions 11-12.

DIRECTIONS: Questions 11 and 12 are to be answered SOLELY on the basis of the information contained in the following quotation.

The coordination of the many activities of a large public agency is absolutely essential. Coordination, as an administrative principle, must be distinguished from and is independent of cooperation. Coordination can be of either the horizontal or the vertical type. In large organizations, the objectives of vertical coordination are achieved by the transmission of orders and statements of policy down through the various levels of authority. It is an accepted generalization that the more authoritarian the organization, the more easily may vertical coordination be accomplished. Horizontal coordination is arrived at through staff work, administrative management, and conferences of administrators of equal rank. It is obvious that of the two types of coordination, the vertical kind is more important, for at best horizontal coordination only supplements the coordination effected up and down the line.

11. According to the above quotation, the ease with which vertical coordination is achieved in a large agency depends upon the

    A. extent to which control is firmly exercised from above
    B. objectives that have been established for the agency
    C. importance attached by employees to the orders and statements of policy transmitted through the agency
    D. cooperation obtained at the various levels of authority

12. According to the above quotation,

    A. vertical coordination is dependent for its success upon horizontal coordination
    B. one type of coordination may work in opposition to the other
    C. similar methods may be used to achieve both types of coordination
    D. horizontal coordination is at most an addition to vertical coordination

13. In a public agency, standards of work performance may be established more easily for some types of work than for others.
    Of the following types of work, the one which would lend itself MOST readily to the establishment of standards of performance is that done by a(n)

    A. clerk who is assigned to give information to visitors to the agency
    B. stenographer to a bureau chief who performs all his secretarial work
    C. clerk assigned to compute employee withholding tax deductions
    D. accountant who is assigned to examine the records of private firms doing business with the agency

14. *When a supervisor issues an order assigning a task to a subordinate, it is advisable to point out the facts or conditions that have made the order necessary.*
    Of the following, the LEAST valid justification for telling a subordinate why an order is issued is to

    A. avoid giving the subordinate the impression that the order is an arbitrary one
    B. give the subordinate a sense of responsibility in connection with the task to be done
    C. show the subordinate how the task fits into the work of the unit
    D. delegate to the subordinate final responsibility for seeing that the work is done properly

15. Of the following, the CHIEF value of an organization chart of a public agency is that such a chart

    A. limits and defines the functions and procedures of each division in the agency
    B. indicates the lines of authority and responsibility existing in the agency
    C. facilitates the flow of work among divisions in the agency
    D. assists the management of the agency in administering the funds allocated to the agency

16. Assume that you are the head of a central stenographic unit that serves a large number of clerks who answer routine inquiries from the public. You notice that many of the letters of reply dictated by these clerks are almost identical.
    Of the following, the MOST efficient course of action for you to take in connection with this matter is to

    A. assign one of your subordinates to specialize in typing these letters
    B. reduce the monotony of the work by dividing it evenly among the stenographers in the unit
    C. suggest to your stenographers that these letters be typed at one time after a sufficient number have been accumulated
    D. recommend the preparation of a form letter to be used in answering this correspondence

17. As the supervisor of a small unit, you have assigned one of your subordinates to file papers for several hours each day.
    Of the following, the MOST important factor that you should consider in evaluating the quantity of work done by this subordinate when he is filing is that

    A. filing is a monotonous, routine task that discourages an employee from doing his best work
    B. objective standards for measuring work done in filing are difficult to develop
    C. the number of pieces of material which can be filed in a given amount of time varies with the nature of the material filed
    D. the time spent on filing papers may be reduced by standardizing the size of material filed

18. As supervisor of a central stenographic unit, you are about to change the procedures used in your unit for filing various types of material.
    The MOST important reason why you should ask your subordinates for comments and suggestions on any changes in procedures before putting these changes into effect is that

    A. your subordinates may make constructive suggestions based on their familiarity with the work
    B. the subordinates who submit constructive suggestions can be given adequate recognition for their contributions
    C. procedures are most effective when they are phrased in the language used on the job
    D. your subordinates may obtain a better understanding of the scope of your duties and responsibilities

19. *A governmental agency may establish and maintain certain types of communications for use primarily within its own organization. These communications are intended to be directed primarily to persons who are members of that organization, or subject to that organization's authority and control, and represent what is sometimes called "administrative communication".*
On the basis of this quotation, the one of the following which may NOT properly be called an example of administrative communication is that of

    A. an administrative assistant issuing a press release to a newspaper reporter
    B. a unit supervisor issuing written instructions to his subordinates for carrying out a long-range assignment
    C. the personnel officer of an agency issuing a memorandum to the employees of the agency listing changes in annual and sick leave regulations
    D. the head of an agency issuing an announcement to the staff concerning a new suggestion system

20. Suppose that you are the supervisor of a central transcribing unit. You have been given a complex assignment for your stenographers to do according to a specific, complicated procedure, and which they must begin work on immediately. This assignment requires about one week for completion and is to be done henceforth every three months. Of the following, the MOST efficient technique for you to use in instructing your stenographers in the procedure to be followed in doing this assignment is for you to

    A. give complete oral instructions to the unit the first time the assignment is to be done and answer individual questions when the assignment is repeated
    B. withhold the assignment for several days until you can prepare complete written instructions for your stenographers
    C. give complete oral instructions to each stenographer every time the assignment is to be done
    D. give complete oral instructions the first time the assignment is to be done and issue complete written instructions for your stenographers to refer to when they perform the assignment again

21. *A primary objective of an office supervisor is to obtain at least standard performance from all the employees in his unit, that is, performance comparable to that which would be expected from a satisfactory, competent employee.* When the supervisor of a large stenographic unit notices that one of his subordinates consistently exceeds the performance standards set for the unit, it is MOST logical for the supervisor FIRST to

    A. commend this subordinate for her work achievements
    B. examine the performance standards set for the unit to determine whether they should be changed
    C. encourage this subordinate by giving her more varied assignments
    D. have this subordinate show other employees of the unit how to increase their production

22. The flow of work in a public agency may be impeded by a number of factors. Some of the factors impeding the flow of work may be controlled or corrected more easily than others. Of the following, the factor impeding flow of work which is MOST difficult for a public agency to control is

A. a lack of adequate standards of performance
B. unexpected changes in the volume of work
C. unforeseen vacation requests by employees
D. assignment of employees without considering their abilities

23. In some modern offices, desks are so arranged that the employees of a unit sit with their backs to their supervisors.
Of the following, the MOST justifiable purpose for this arrangement is to

    A. enable the supervisor to see what each of his subordinates is doing
    B. permit the supervisor to receive visitors with a minimum of disturbance to his employees
    C. enable employees to converse with each other without disturbing the supervisor
    D. expedite the smooth flow of work from the supervisor to each of his subordinates

24. *The work production of typists is sometimes measured by the number of strokes typed per unit of time.*
This method of work measurement is

    A. *desirable* because the total number of strokes counted may disclose improper use of the space bar
    B. *undesirable* because the total number of strokes may be counted incorrectly if a typist is typing too slowly or too quickly
    C. *desirable* when subjective, as well as objective, factors must be taken into account
    D. *undesirable* when there is wide variation in the complexity of the material typed

25. Assume that you have been assigned to assist in the revision and improvement of office forms used by the employees in your agency.
Of the following, the MOST important principle for you to follow in this assignment is that

    A. use of the forms should be confined to as few employees as possible
    B. enough information should be recorded on the forms to make references to other office records unnecessary
    C. a standard procedure should be set up to insure that the revised forms contain the same titles and form numbers as the forms they replace
    D. the recording of information on the forms and the handling of the forms should be simplified as much as possible

26. As supervisor of a stenographic unit, you assign one of your stenographers to type a long, complicated report. After she begins work on the report, she asks you to explain the procedure to be followed in preparing a part of the report. You explain the procedure, but realize later that you have omitted instructions which she should have been given.
Of the following, the MOST appropriate action for you to take in this situation is to

    A. state that you gave her incomplete instructions and supply her with the instructions you omitted
    B. suggest, without referring to your omission, that she use her judgment in handling problems not covered by your instructions
    C. supply her with the additional instructions when it becomes apparent that she is preparing the report incorrectly
    D. assure the stenographer that you will answer any further questions she may have about this assignment

27. A supervisor administering on-the-job training to a new employee can make this training effective by correcting the errors that the employee makes in his work.
   To make the training effective, it would be MOST appropriate for the supervisor to correct the employee's errors

   A. as soon as possible after the errors have become serious
   B. after the employee has been given time to discover and correct his errors himself
   C. as soon as practicable after the errors have been discovered
   D. in work review sessions scheduled at montly intervals

Questions 28-37.

DIRECTION: Each of Questions 28 through 37 consists of two sentences. Either or both of these sentences may contain errors in grammar, sentence structure, or punctuation, or both sentences may be correct. Indicate your answer in the space at the right as follows:
If only Sentence I contains an error, print the letter A;
If only Sentence II contains an error, print the letter B;
If both sentences contain errors, print the letter C;
If both sentences are correct, print the letter D.

28. I. The task of typing these reports is to be divided equally between you and me.
    II. If I was he, I would use a different method for filing these records.

29. I. The new clerk is just as capable as some of the older employees, if not more capable.
    II. Using his knowledge of arithmetic to check the calculations, the supervisor found no errors in the report.

30. I. A typist who does consistently superior work probably merits promotion.
    II. In its report on the stenographic unit, the committee pointed out that neither the stenographers nor the typists were adequately trained.

31. I. Entering the office, the desk was noticed immediately by the visitor.
    II. Arrangements have been made to give this training to whoever applies for it.

32. I. The office manager estimates that this assignment, which is to be handled by you and I, will require about two weeks for completion.
    II. One of the recommendations of the report is that these kind of forms be discarded because they are of no value.

33. I. The supervisor knew that the typist was a quiet, cooperative, efficient, employee.
    II. The duties of a stenographer are to take dictation notes at conferences and transcribing them.

34. I. The stenographer has learned that she, as well as two typists, is being assigned to the new unit.
    II. We do not know who you have designated to take charge of the new program.

35. I. He asked, "When do you expect to return?"
    II. I doubt whether this system will be successful here; it is not suitable for the work of our agency.

36. I. It is a policy of this agency to encourage punctuality as a good habit for we employ- 36._____
ees to adopt.
II. The successful completion of the task was due largely to them cooperating
effectively with the supervisor.

37. I. Mr. Smith, who is a very competent executive has offered his services to our 37._____
department.
II. Every one of the stenographers who work in this office is considered trustworthy.

Questions 38-47.

DIRECTIONS: Each of Questions 38 through 47 consists of four words. In each question, one of the words may be spelled incorrectly or all four words may be spelled correctly. If one of the words in a question is spelled incorrectly, print in the space at the right the capital letter preceding the word which is spelled incorrectly. If all four words are spelled correctly, print the letter E.

38. A. dismissal   B. collateral   38._____
    C. leisure   D. proffession

39. A. subsidary   B. outrageous   39._____
    C. liaison   D. assessed

40. A. already   B. changeable   40._____
    C. mischevous   D. cylinder

41. A. supersede   B. deceit   41._____
    C. dissension   D. imminent

42. A. arguing   B. contagious   42._____
    C. comparitive   D. accessible

43. A. indelible   B. existance   43._____
    C. presumptuous   D. mileage

44. A. extention   B. aggregate   44._____
    C. sustenance   D. gratuitous

45. A. interrogate   B. exaggeration   45._____
    C. vacillate   D. moreover

46. A. parallel   B. derogatory   46._____
    C. admissable   D. appellate

47. A. safety   B. cumalative   47._____
    C. disappear   D. usable

48. In 2005, a city agency bought 12,000 envelopes at 40 cents per hundred. In 2006, the 48._____
price of envelopes purchased was 40 percent higher than the 2005 price, but only 60
percent as many envelopes were bought.
The total cost of the envelopes purchased in 2006 was MOST NEARLY

   A. $25   B. $32   C. $40   D. $48

49. In a city agency, 25 percent of the women employees and 50 percent of the men employees attended a general staff meeting.
If 48 percent of all the employees in the agency are women, the percentage of all the employees who attended the meeting is

    A. 36%   B. 37%   C. 38%   D. 75%

Questions 50-66.

DIRECTIONS: Each of Questions 50 through 66 consists of a word in capitals followed by four suggested meanings of the word. Print in the space at the right the letter preceding the word which means MOST NEARLY the same as the word in capitals.

50. ATTRITION
    A. expansion   B. competition
    C. wearing down   D. complete agreement

51. PROPONENT
    A. advocate   B. predecessor
    C. critic   D. recipient

52. AFFLUENCE
    A. extent   B. competence
    C. prestige   D. wealth

53. INVIOLATE
    A. negative
    B. incapable of
    C. unimpaired
    D. contrary to accepted procedures

54. SUCCINCT
    A. full   B. helpful
    C. misleading   D. concise

55. DELINEATE
    A. consider   B. describe   C. curtail   D. develop

56. SUPERCILIOUS
    A. contemptuous   B. significant
    C. indirect   D. spiteful

57. INCULCATE
    A. demonstrate   B. prove wrong
    C. instill   D. enlarge gradually

58. PALPABLE
    A. favorable   B. obvious
    C. fortunate   D. deceptive

59. STIGMA   59.____
    A. discord   B. blemish
    C. deviation   D. belief

60. COPIOUS   60.____
    A. accurate   B. well-written
    C. current   D. plentiful

61. PERSPICACITY   61.____
    A. discernment   B. ambition
    C. boldness   D. reputation

62. RECALCITRANT   62.____
    A. responsible   B. obstinate
    C. indignant   D. vague

63. INVEIGLE   63.____
    A. entice   B. absorb   C. introduce   D. permit

64. INCONGRUOUS   64.____
    A. minor   B. balanced
    C. inconsistent   D. unsympathetic

65. ADAMANT   65.____
    A. original   B. kind
    C. inflexible   D. cowardly

66. TRITE   66.____
    A. common   B. offensive
    C. coarse   D. excessive

67. ELICIT   67.____
    A. act illegally   B. draw forth
    C. expect   D. erase

68. AUGMENT   68.____
    A. review   B. arrange   C. increase   D. accept

Questions 69-73.

DIRECTIONS: Each of Questions 69 through 73 consists of four words which are to be divided at the end of a typewritten line. One word in each question is divided incorrectly. For each question, indicate in the space at the right the letter preceding the word which is divided incorrectly.

69. A. prohib-itive   B. inter-rupted   69.____
    C. simpli-fied   D. except-ion

70. A. pass-ing   B. expen-sive   70.____
    C. ann-ual   D. adminis-ter

71. A. neces-sary B. essent-ial 71.____
    C. excel-lent D. ordi-nary

72. A. add-ress B. identi-cal 72.____
    C. prop-erly D. flex-ible

73. A. furi-ous B. pro-vide 73.____
    C. anx-ious D. compell-ing

Questions 74-80.

DIRECTIONS: Questions 74 through 80 are to be answered on the basis of the chart on the following page. This chart contains three curves which connect the points that show for each week the percentage of time spent by stenographers in a central stenographic unit in Department X on taking shorthand notes, typing, and filing for a ten-week period.

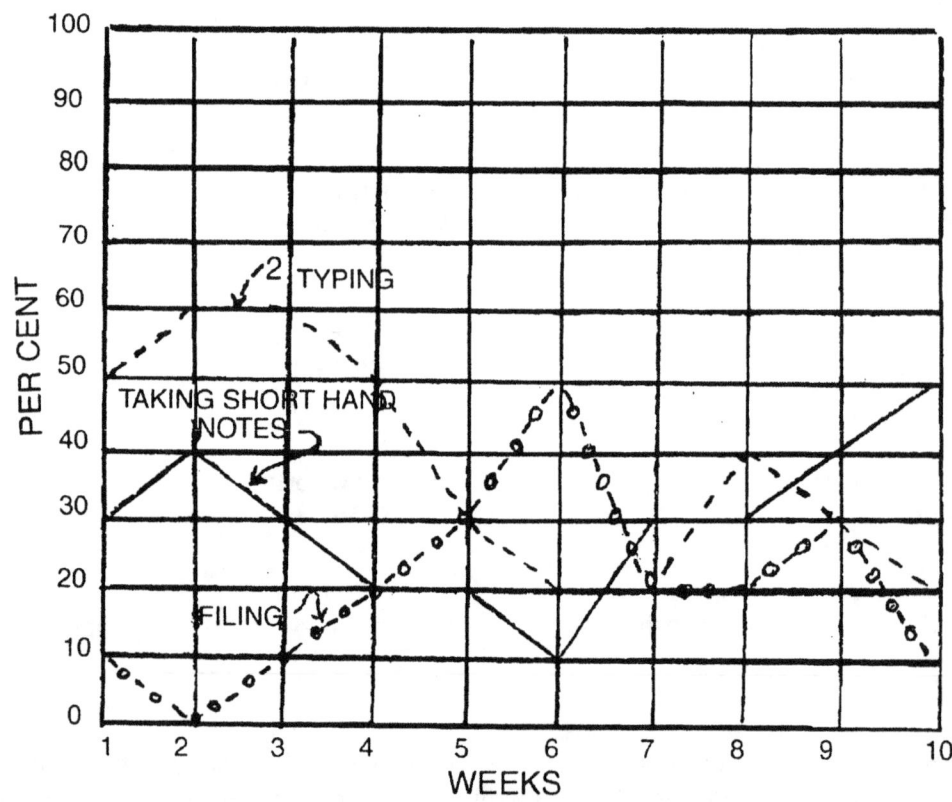

CENTRAL STENOGRAPHIC UNIT, DEPARTMENT X
Percentage of Time Spent by Stenographers on
Taking Shorthand Notes, Typing, and Filing for
Each Week in a Ten-Week Period

NOTE: Time spent on miscellaneous duties is not indicated on the chart. Where time has been spent on miscellaneous duties in a week, this time may be computed by subtracting from 100 percent the total of the percentage of time spent in typing, filing, and taking shorthand notes, as shown on each curve. Thus, the percentage of time spent on miscellaneous duties in the first week is 10 percent of the total work week.

You are to assume that each employee works 7 hours a day and 5 days a week, making a total of 35 hours for the work week.

Candidates may find it useful to arrange their computations on their scratch paper in an orderly manner since the correct computations for one question may also be helpful in answering another question.

74. Of the following weeks, the one in which there was no change from the preceding week in the percentage of time spent on miscellaneous duties is the _____ week.

    A. fourth   B. fifth   C. sixth   D. seventh

75. For the entire ten-week period, the average percentage of time spent per week on filing is

    A. 20%   B. 18%   C. 22%   D. 14%

76. For the entire ten-week period, the average number of hours spent per week by the typical stenographer on miscellaneous duties is MOST NEARLY _____ hours.

    A. 14   B. 11   C. 6   D. 4

77. For the first five weeks, the average number of hours spent per week by the typical stenographer on taking shorthand notes is MOST NEARLY _____ hours.

    A. 10   B. 8   C. 12   D. 6

78. For the entire ten-week period, the number of hours spent on taking shorthand notes is _____ the number of hours spent on filing.

    A. equal to
    B. 50% greater than
    C. 67% greater than
    D. 33% less than

79. In the week in which the percentage of time spent on miscellaneous duties is the greatest, the percentage of time spent on _____ than the percentage of time spent on typing.

    A. filing is greater
    B. taking shorthand notes is less
    C. typing is greater
    D. taking shorthand notes is greater

80. Assume that the staff as a whole files an average of 600 papers per hour during the time spent on filing. Then, the total number of papers filed during the entire ten-week period is

    A. 4,200   B. 8,400   C. 42,000   D. 84,000

KEY (CORRECT ANSWERS)

1.	D	21.	A	41.	E	61.	A
2.	C	22.	B	42.	C	62.	B
3.	D	23.	B	43.	B	63.	A
4.	B	24.	D	44.	A	64.	C
5.	D	25.	D	45.	E	65.	C
6.	B	26.	A	46.	C	66.	A
7.	C	27.	C	47.	B	67.	B
8.	A	28.	B	48.	C	68.	C
9.	B	29.	D	49.	C	69.	D
10.	C	30.	D	50.	C	70.	C
11.	A	31.	A	51.	A	71.	B
12.	D	32.	C	52.	D	72.	A
13.	C	33.	C	53.	C	73.	D
14.	D	34.	B	54.	D	74.	C
15.	B	35.	D	55.	B	75.	A
16.	D	36.	C	56.	A	76.	D
17.	C	37.	A	57.	C	77.	A
18.	A	38.	D	58.	B	78.	B
19.	A	39.	A	59.	B	79.	D
20.	D	40.	C	60.	D	80.	C

EXAMINATION SECTION
TEST 1

DIRECTIONS: Each question or incomplete statement is followed by several suggested answers or completions. Select the one that BEST answers the question or completes the statement. *PRINT THE LETTER OF THE CORRECT ANSWER IN THE SPACE AT THE RIGHT.*

1. Assume that you are the supervisor of a stenographic unit. One of your stenographers, in reviewing her stenographic notes of a letter dictated by a bureau head, discovers that the letter contains an erroneous statement which may cause the bureau head some embarrassment. Since the stenographer had been severely criticized by this bureau head on a previous occasion for having re-phrased one of his dictated statements, she is reluctant to make any changes in his dictated material. She refers this problem to you.
   Under these circumstances, the BEST action for you to take is to

   A. correct the error and have the stenographer type the letter as corrected, after you have initialed her notebook to show that you have authorized the change
   B. have the stenographer type the letter as it was dictated by the bureau head, but have her attach a note calling his attention to the erroneous statement
   C. have the stenographer transcribe the letter as dictated, except for the erroneous statement; instruct her to leave a blank space for the insertion of a revised statement
   D. call the bureau head's attention to this error and have the stenographer make any change authorized by him

1.____

2. Suppose you are requested to write a report explaining the value of compiling a manual of procedure for use by the stenographers under your supervision.
   Of the following, the CHIEF justification you can give for compiling such a manual is that

   A. further revisions of procedures will be unnecessary once a standardized manual is completed and approved
   B. it will contain information which you might otherwise have to communicate orally to your subordinates
   C. fundamental rules of grammar and letter writing should be in readily available form
   D. your subordinates will not have to ask you any questions

2.____

3. Suppose that you are required to prepare a report evaluating the services of the stenographers you supervise.
   Of the following, the stenographer who should be considered LEAST capable is the one who

   A. stated that she could not work overtime when requested on several occasions to do so
   B. was dissatisfied with the nature of the work assigned to her
   C. attempted on several occasions to procure a transfer to another department
   D. was unable to follow instructions in the performance of routine duties

3.____

117

4. As a secretary to a division chief, you may receive requests for information which you know should not be divulged.
   Of the following replies you may give to such a request received over the telephone, the BEST one is:

   A. I regret to advise you that it is the policy of the department not to give out this information over the telephone
   B. If you hold on a moment, I'll have you connected with the chief of the division
   C. I am sorry that I cannot help you, but we are not permitted to give out any information regarding such matters
   D. I am sorry, but I know nothing regarding this matter

5. The stenographer should be well-grounded in the rules underlying the best usage of English.
   Of the following, the BEST justification for this statement is that

   A. the majority of stenographers today are high school graduates
   B. a stenographer's responsibility goes beyond mere transcription of dictated material
   C. a stenographer engaged in transcription is not usually aware of major imperfections in sentence structure
   D. laws governing correct English usage are rarely modified

6. Of the following, the LEAST justifiable reason for the establishment of a central transcribing unit is that

   A. confidential assignments can be more closely guarded
   B. the quantity of work done can be more easily measured
   C. the work can be more equally distributed
   D. supervisory costs can be decreased

7. Suppose that you are the secretary to Mr. Smith, the administrative official who is responsible for securing special equipment, supplies, and services for your department. In carrying out his duties, Mr. Smith interviews agents of companies interested in having your department utilize their products and services. You have been informed by Mr. Smith that he does not wish to see certain agents.
   The BEST one of the following methods which you may use in denying an interview to one of these unwelcome representatives is to

   A. inform him frankly and bluntly that Mr. Smith has left specific instructions that certain agents are not to be granted interviews
   B. tell him that Mr. Smith has left the office and will not return that day
   C. take his calling card, note the reason for his call, and then tell him that he will be notified by mail or telephone when Mr. Smith wishes to see him
   D. make a note of the nature of his business, then inform him that Mr. Smith will be busy for the remainder of that day and request him to return to the office at a later date

8. Of the following procedures, the MOST effective one for you, as the supervisor of a transcribing unit, to follow is to

   A. assign the more difficult tasks to those typists who are careless in their work
   B. allow typists possessing superior abilities to set up their own standards of performance

C. rank your subordinates according to their coopera-tiveness and make all assignments on the basis of this rating
D. make sure that your subordinates clearly understand the instructions for performing the tasks assigned to them

9. Training promotes cooperation and teamwork and results in lowered unit costs of operation.
   The one of the following which is the MOST valid implication of the above statement is that

   A. training is of most value to new employees
   B. training is a factor in increasing efficiency and morale
   C. the actual cost of training employees may be small
   D. training is unnecessary in offices where personnel costs cannot be reduced

10. A city employee should understand how his particular duties contribute to the achievement of the objectives of his department.
    This statement means MOST NEARLY that

    A. an employee who understands the functions of his department will perform his work efficiently
    B. all employees contribute equally in carrying out the objectives of their department
    C. an employee should realize the significance of his work in relation to the aims of his department
    D. all employees should be able to assist in setting up the objectives of a department

11. In introducing a major change in the method of performing an important clerical operation, the office supervisor should FIRST

    A. demonstrate this new method to his employees
    B. have his employees try out the new method under his supervision; he should then correct any errors they make
    C. have his most capable subordinate demonstrate the new method to the other employees
    D. inform his employees of the reason, or reasons, for adopting the change in the method

12. To determine the productivity of the office worker, one must look beyond the particular piece of work done and consider the result that is accomplished. If there is no useful result, there is no product, and, in such a case, the employee is to be considered a non-producer. On the basis of this statement, it is MOST accurate to conclude that

    A. where two employees are performing similar types of work, one may be unproductive and the other productive
    B. an employee who performs a given task effectively must necessarily be considered a productive worker
    C. the product of a typist is the typewritten material she has prepared
    D. office workers are usually less productive than factory workers

13. Assume that you are the head of a central stenographic unit from which stenographers are assigned to different units of the department as needed. On one occasion, a unit head sends you a note concerning the work of Jane Roe, one of your stenographers, which states as follows: *Miss Roe is very inefficient; please do not assign her to me in the future.*
Of the following, the BEST action for you to take FIRST is to

    A. show the note to the stenographer but make no comment
    B. give her special training in the various phases of a stenographer's job
    C. tell the stenographer that she must improve her work
    D. determine in what way the stenographer's work has been inefficient

14. Scheduling work within a unit requires a knowledge of the length of time it takes to perform the component parts of a task and of the precedence which certain tasks should take over others.
The one of the following which is the MOST valid implication of this statement is that

    A. the priority which is given some tasks over others is determined by the length of time it takes to perform the component parts of each task
    B. only those tasks can be scheduled which have been performed in the unit in the past
    C. some tasks in a unit do not have component parts
    D. in order to estimate the time required to complete an assignment, a knowledge of the rate of performance of each part of the assignment is necessary

15. Many office managers have a tendency to overuse form letters and are prone to print form letters for every occasion, regardless of the number of copies of these letters which is needed.
On the basis of this statement, it is MOST logical to state that the determination of the need for a form letter should depend upon the

    A. length of the period during which the form letter may be used
    B. number of form letters presently being used in the office
    C. frequency with which the form letter may be used
    D. number of typists who may use the form letter

16. The head of a central transcribing unit has prepared monthly reports of the total amount of work performed by her unit.
An analysis of the monthly reports for twenty-four successive months would be of LEAST value to the unit head in

    A. anticipating peak work-load periods
    B. determining the quality of work which she can expect each employee to perform in the future
    C. determining future personnel needs
    D. estimating the amount of supplies that will be needed for the ensuing year

17. When asked to comment upon the efficiency of Miss Smith, a stenographer, her supervisor said, *Since she rarely makes an error, I consider her very efficient.*
Of the following, the MOST valid assumption underlying this supervisor's comment is that

A. speed and accuracy should be considered separately in evaluating a stenographer's efficiency
B. the most accurate stenographers are not necessarily the most efficient
C. accuracy and competency are directly related
D. accuracy is largely dependent upon the intelligence of a stenographer

18. Suppose that you are in charge of a central filing unit in your department. In order to provide additional space for current file materials, you recently transferred a large amount of file material from the active files to the storage files. You notice that your file clerks are spending a considerable amount of time in fulfilling requests for reports recently transferred to the storage files.
Of the following steps you might take to remedy this situation, the BEST one for you to take FIRST is to

    A. examine the reports requested as a possible aid in determining what portion of the stored material should be returned to the active files
    B. transfer back to the active files only those reports for which you have received requests; the balance of the file material is to be kept in the storage files
    C. have all the material recently transferred to the storage files returned to the active files; requisition additional file cabinets for current file materials
    D. determine the date of the report bearing the earliest date and return to the active file all reports bearing that date and later dates

19. The successful supervisor wins his victories through preventive rather than through curative action.
The one of the following which is the MOST accurate interpretation on the basis of this statement is that

    A. success in supervision may be measured more accurately in terms of errors corrected than in terms of errors prevented
    B. anticipating problems makes for better supervision than waiting until these problems arise
    C. difficulties that cannot be prevented by the supervisor cannot be overcome
    D. the solution of problems in supervision is best achieved by scientific methods

20. Assume that you have been requested to design an office form which is to be duplicated. In planning the layout of the various items appearing on the form, it is LEAST important for you to know the

    A. amount of information which the form is to contain
    B. purpose for which the form will be used
    C. size of the form
    D. number of copies of the form which are required

21. Assume you are typing a letter which includes a quotation of several consecutive paragraphs. You should place quotation marks _____ paragraph quoted.

    A. at the beginning and end of each
    B. at the beginning of each paragraph quoted and at the end of the last
    C. *only* at the beginning of the first paragraph quoted and at the end of the last
    D. *only* at the beginning of each

22. The supervisor of a large central typing bureau is responsible for the accuracy of the work performed by her subordinates.
    Of the following procedures which she might adopt to insure the accurate copying of long reports from rough draft originals, the MOST effective one is to

    A. examine the rough draft for errors in grammar, punctuation, and spelling before assigning it to a typist to copy
    B. glance through each typed report before it leaves her bureau to detect any obvious errors made by the typist
    C. have another employee read the rough draft original to the typist who typed the report, and have the typist make whatever corrections are necessary
    D. rotate assignments involving the typing of long reports equally among all the typists in the unit

22.____

23. The total number of errors made during the month, or other period studied, indicates, in a general way, whether the work has been performed with reasonable accuracy. However, this is not in itself a true measure, but must be considered in relation to the total volume of work produced.
    On the basis of this statement, the accuracy of work performed in a central stenographic unit is MOST truly measured by the

    A. total number of errors made during a specific period
    B. comparison of the number of errors made during one month with the number made during the preceding month
    C. ratio between the number of errors made and the quantity of work produced during a specified period
    D. average amount of work produced by the unit during each month or other designated period of time

23.____

24. Assume that a new stenographer, Maria Gonzalez, has been assigned to work under your supervision and is reporting to work for the first time. You formally introduce Maria to her co-workers and suggest that a few of the other typists explain the office procedures and typing formats to her.
    The practice of instructing Maria in her duties in this manner is

    A. *good,* because she will be made to feel at home
    B. *good,* because she will learn more about routine office tasks from co-workers than from you
    C. *poor,* because her co-workers will resent the extra work
    D. *poor,* because you will not have enough control over her training

24.____

25. The supervisor you assist is under great pressure to meet certain target dates. He has scheduled an emergency meeting to take place in a few days, and he asks you to send out notices immediately. As you begin to prepare the notices, however, you realize he has scheduled the meeting for a Saturday, which is not a working day. Also, you sense that your supervisor is not in a good mood. Which of the following is the MOST effective method of handling this situation?

    A. Change the meeting date to the first working day after that Saturday and send out the notices.
    B. Change the meeting date to a working day on which his calendar is clear and send out the notices.
    C. Point out to your supervisor that the date is a Saturday.
    D. Send out the notices as they are, since you have received specific instructions.

25.____

KEY (CORRECT ANSWERS)

1.	D	11.	D
2.	B	12.	A
3.	D	13.	D
4.	C	14.	D
5.	B	15.	C
6.	A	16.	B
7.	C	17.	C
8.	D	18.	A
9.	B	19.	B
10.	C	20.	D

21. B
22. C
23. C
24. D
25. C

COURT REPORTING

SOUNDS

A. **SHORT VOWELS**

It is now time for you to hear the distinct difference between words having SHORT VOWEL SOUNDS and words having LONG VOWEL SOUNDS.

The following word list of SHORT VOWEL SOUNDS are to be said out loud. Read the word. "Hear" the SHORT VOWEL SOUND. See how it is written on the machine. Write each word followed by the "Period" stroke –FPLT.

Sound	Word	Machine	Written
A	cat	A	KAT
	hat	A	HAT
	pad	A	PAD
	bad	A	BAD
	pan	A	PAN
	fan	A	FAN
E	bed	E	BED
	head	E	HED
	tell	E	TEL
	well	E	WEL
	set	E	SET
	get	E	GET
I	sit	EU	SEUT
	hit	EU	HEUT
	pin	EU	PEUN
	win	EU	WEUN
	fill	EU	FEUL
	bill	EU	BEUL
O	lot	AU	LAUT
	hot	AU	HAUT
	rod	AU	NAUD
	nod	AU	NAUD
	tall	AU	TAUL
	ball	AU	BAUL
U	love	U	LUV
	dove	U	DUV
	cuff	U	KUF
	stuff	U	STUF
	tough	U	TUF
	rough	U	RUF

Read your notes OUT LOUD. Repeat 20 times.

B. **LONG VOWELS**

It is now time to hear the LONG VOWEL SOUNDS.

The following word list of LONG VOWEL SOUNDS are to be said out loud. Read the word. "Hear" the LONG VOWEL SOUND. See how it is written on the machine. Write each word followed by the "Period" stroke –FPLT.

Sound	Word	Machine	Written
A	late	AEU	LAEUT
	rate	AEU	RAEUT
	made	AEU	MAEUD
	paid	AEU	PAEUD
	cane	AEU	KAEUN
	lane	AEU	LAEUN
E	meet	AE	MAET
	beat	AE	BAET
	deed	AE	DAED
	need	AE	NAED
	lean	AE	LAEN
	seen	AE	SAEN
I	kite	AOEU	KAOEUT
	bite	AOEU	BAOEUT
	time	AOEU	TAOEUM
	dime	AOEU	DAOEUM
	file	AOEU	FAOEUL
	mile	AOEU	MAOEUL
O	snow	OE	SNOE
	row	OE	ROE
	coat	OE	KOET
	wrote	OE	ROET
	load	OE	LOED
	road	OE	ROED
U	flue	AO	FLAO
	new	AO	NAO
	food	AO	FAOD
	rude	AO	RAOD
	soon	AO	SAON
	tune	AO	TAON

Read your notes OUT LOUD. Repeat 20 times.

C. **OTHER SOUNDS**

The following SOUNDS should be said OUT LOUD for you to hear for the very first time.

Say each word OUT LOUD before writing it on the machine. Write each word followed by the "Period" stroke –FPLT.

Sound	Word	Machine	Written
"OW"	how	OU	HOU
	now	OU	NOU
	brown	OU	BROUN
"AW"	job	AU	JAUB
	pawn	AU	PAUN
	taught	AU	TAUT
"OY"	boy	OEU	BOEU
	toy	OEU	TOEU
	ploy	OEU	PLOEU
"OI"	toil	OEU	TOEUL
	coin	OEU	KOEUN
	void	OEU	VOEUD

Read your notes OUT LOUD. Repeat 20 times.

C. **OTHER SOUNDS**

The following SOUNDS need to be said OUT LOUD very slowly and very distinctly before writing them on the machine.

Be sure to HEAR the SOUNDS as you are writing the outlines. Write each word followed by the "Period" stroke –FPLT.

Sound	Word	Machine	Written
"OO"	look	O	LOK
	took	O	TOK
	cook	O	KOK
	put	O	POT
	soot	O	SOT
	wood	O	WOD
	hood	O	HOD
	push	O	POSH
	bush	O	BOSH

Read your notes OUT LOUD. Repeat 20 times.

4

The following words SOUND alike. Be sure to HEAR the SOUNDS as you write them on the machine. Write each word followed by the "Period" stroke –FPLT.

Sound	Word	Machine	Written
"OOL"	cool	U	KUL
	tool	U	TUL
	school	U	SKUL
"UL"	pull	U	PUL
	bull	U	BUL
	full	U	FUL

Read your notes OUT LOUD. Repeat 20 times.

The following SOUND is very distinct. HEAR the SOUND as you are writing it on the machine. Write each word followed by the "Period" stroke –FPLT.

Sound	Word	Machine	Written
"AR"	art	AR	ART
	car	AR	KAR
	mark	AR	MARK
	hard	AR	HARD
	bar	AR	BAR
	guard	AR	GARD

Read your notes OUT LOUD. Repeat 20 times.

The following SOUNDS are very similar. Say the SOUNDS very slowly OUT LOUD and be sure to HEAR the SOUNDS as you are writing the outlines. Write each word followed by the "Period" stroke –FPLT.

Sound	Word	Machine	Written
"IR"	sir	EUR	SEUR
	girl	EUR	GEURL
	flirt	EUR	FLEURT
"ER"	jerk	EUR	JEURK
	term	EUR	TEURM
	herd	EUR	HEURD
"UR"	turn	EUR	TEURN
	lurk	EUR	LEURK
	purse	EUR	PEURS
"WUR"	world	UR	WURLD
	work	UR	WURK
	word	UR	WURD

Read your notes OUT LOUD. Repeat 20 times.

The following SOUNDS are the "stressed" LONG VOWEL SOUNDS of the "U" SOUND. Although these words are few in number, there is a need for distinction in the writing outline.

EXAMPLE: WHO and HUE
WHO has the LONG VOWEL SOUND of "U"
HUE has the "stressed" LONG VOWEL SOUND of "U"

These words are written as differently and as distinctly as their two SOUNDS dictate:

WHO is written: HAO
HUE is written: HAOU

Say the following words OUT LOUD very slowly and distinctly before writing that word on the machine. Be sure to HEAR the SOUNDS as you are writing the outlines. Write each word followed by the "Period" stroke –FPLT.

Sound	Word	Machine	Written
"UU—"	hue	AOU	HAOU
	cue	AOU	KAOU
	queue	AOU	KAOU
	fued	AOU	FAOUD
	fuel	AOU	FAOUL
	mule	AOU	MAOUL
	cute	AOU	KAOUT
	cube	AOU	KAOUB
	few	AOU	FAOU
	view	AOU	VAOU
	hew	AOU	HAOU
	pew	AOU	PAOU
	fuse	AOU	FAOUZ
	muse	AOU	MAOUZ
	mute	AOU	MAOUT
	puke	AOU	PAOUK
	pure	AOU	PAOUR
	cure	AOU	KAOUR

Read your notes OUT LOUD. Repeat 20 times.

6

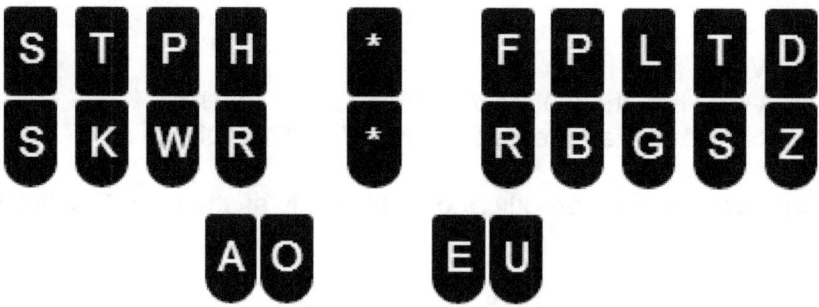

It is now time for you to learn the "Underscore" stroke. Simply stroke all the LOWER KEYS on the INITIAL and FINAL sides of the keyboard together:

        S – K – W – R   R – B – G – S

This is your "Underscore" stroke. LEARN IT WELL.

The "Underscore" stroke is used immediately after you have written a Proper Name. This SKWR RBGS outline tells you that the stroke or strokes immediately preceding it are to be capitalized.

EXAMPLE: J A U N
                     M A E U
                     S K W R R B G S

The "Underscore" stroke tells you that the preceding outlines are to be capitalized as: John May.

As you can see, if you DID NOT "Underscore" immediately after the Proper Name, the word "may" could become very confused within the sentence and make readability extremely difficult.

The Rule is: <u>ALWAYS</u> UNDERSCORE A PROPER NAME.

Also, the "Underscore" stroke can be used to denoted something unusual in your writing, such as an unfamiliar word, a foreign word, a slang word, etc. The "Underscore" stroke signals you that the preceding outline demands your special attention.

The "Underscore" stroke is your friend. USE IT WELL.

MOST COMMON WORDS

For our beginner's learning process, I have selected 100 of the commoner words for practice. They are listed in high usage sequence.

Write each word followed by the "Period" stroke –FPLT.

	WORD	WRITTEN		WORD	WRITTEN
1.	it	EUT	26.	some	SUM
2.	was	WAUZ	27.	great	GRAEUT
3.	as	AZ	28.	such	SUCH
4.	by	BAOEU	29.	first	FEURS
5.	at	AT	30.	how	HOU
6.	all	AUL	31.	come	KUM
7.	one	WUN	32.	us	US
8.	so	SOE	33.	then	THEN
9.	my	MAOEU	34.	like	LAOEUK
10.	me	MAE	35.	well	WEL
11.	war	WOER	36.	little	LEULGTS
12.	more	MOER	37.	say	SAEU
13.	now	NOU	38.	here	HAER
14.	its	EUTS	39.	good	GOD
15.	time	TAOEUM	40.	make	MAEUK
16.	up	UP	41.	most	MOES
17.	out	OUT	42.	way	WAEU
18.	than	THAN	43.	see	SAE
19.	made	MAEUD	44.	world	WURLD
20.	men	MEN	45.	know	NOE
21.	must	MUS	46.	day	DAEU
22.	said	SED	47.	never	NEVR
23.	may	MAEU	48.	new	NAO
24.	man	MAN	49.	down	DOUN
25.	over	OEVR	50.	years	YAERZ

Read your notes OUT LOUD. Repeat 20 times.

Let's continue with the second half.

	WORD	WRITTEN		WORD	WRITTEN
51.	long	LAUNG	76.	per	PEUR
52.	right	RAOEUT	77.	once	WUNS
53.	get	GET	78.	peace	PAES
54.	life	LAOEUF/-F	79.	year	YAER
55.	just	JUS	80.	away	AU/WAEU
56.	take	TAEUK	81.	fact	FAK
57.	work	WURK	82.	half	HAF
58.	things	THEUNGZ	83.	still	STEUL
59.	part	PART	84.	give	GEUV
60.	through	THRAO	85.	power	POUR
61.	while**	WHAOEUL	86.	found	FOUND
62.	last	LA*S	87.	few	FAOU
63.	might	MAOEUT	88.	food	FAOD
64.	back	BAK	89.	house	HOUS
65.	old	OELD	90.	less	LES
66.	own	OEN	91.	oh	OE
67.	came	KAEUM	92.	best	BES
68.	days	DAEUZ	93.	case	KAEUS
69.	yet	YET	94.	line	LAOEUN
70.	same	SAEUM	95.	place	PLAEUS
71.	thought	THAUT	96.	says	SEZ
72.	each	AECH	97.	since	SEUNS
73.	far	FAR	98.	let	LET
74.	home	HOEM	99.	tell	TEL
75.	put	POT	100.	big	BEUG

**The few words in the English language beginning with "WH" should be written on the machine with a beginning "WH" stroke even though the "WH" is not a "true" sound. Examples: white, wheel, wheat, whirl, whistle.

Read your notes OUT LOUD. Repeat 20 times.

REMEMBER: After you have finished practicing the above 100 words, it will be time to again practice them over and over from your "lesson tape" that is made for home practice. To hear the words and all of the SOUNDS is of vital importance.

The Key to Success in learning Reporting is R-E-P-E-T-I-T-I-O-N.

Every time you HEAR a sound and WRITE it into your stenoprint outline, you are programming your computer-brain to accept that sound. Every time you READ your notes, you are programming your computer-brain that these stenoprint outlines are your new language.

If you can READ your notes, you can WRITE your notes. It is as simple as that.

CONNECTING BRIEFS – SENTENCES

Now that your vocabulary on the machine has blossomed within the last few lessons, let's put those words on the machine into SENTENCES.

In order to make SENTENCES, you will need to learn a few CONNECTING BRIEFS at this time.

A. Here are your first ten (10) "High Frequency BRIEF:

INITIAL SIDE	VOWELS	FINAL SIDE
TAO = to	AO = and	-T = the
N- = in	A = a	-F = of
P- = that		-P = that
T- = it (in phrases only)		-S = is
FOER – for		
S- = is		

NOTE: The word "it" is written: EUT.

Read your notes OUT LOUD. Repeat 20 times.

The following are some "High Frequency" PHRASES:

TAOP	=	to that
TAOT	=	to the (Conflict "toot" – very infrequent court word)
N-T	=	in the
P-A	=	that a
P-T	=	that the
P-S	=	that is
T-S	=	it is
FOER-P	=	for that
FOER-T	=	for the (Conflict "fort" – very infrequent court word)
S-A	=	is a
S-P	=	is that
S-T	=	is the
AO-P	=	and that
AO-T	=	and the
-FT	=	of the

Read your notes OUT LOUD. Repeat 20 times.

NOTE: In Dwyer's Simplified Method of Sound Writing, every time there is a Conflict of a BRIEF or a PHRASE in writing, it will be <u>noted</u> and <u>stated</u> exactly what that Conflict is.

You will see it, you will note it, and you will be aware of it.

To put it simply: "To know" of the Conflicts is your key to successful writing and reading.

B. Now, let's READ SENTENCES OUT LOUD.

> NOTE: When the word "is" stands alone, it may be written with either the INITIAL S or the FINAL S.
>
> When the word "that" stands alone, it may be written with either the INITIAL P or the FINAL P.

WUN FPLT T-S KWAOEUT A NOEN FAK P-T STAEUT –S RAOEUT FPLT

TO FPLT –T HOEL THEUNG KAEM OUT N-T MEULGTS –FT STOER FPLT

THRE FPLT AUFN T-S KAULD A BALGTS FOERT KAUZ FPLT

FOR FPLT –T DAER LEULGTS KHAOEULD –S N-T FRUNT –FT HOUS FPLT

FAOEUV FPLT KAUL MAE AO SAEU –T AUL –T RAUNG –S N-T PA*S FPLT

SEUX FPLT AECH MAN –S TAO TAEUK LAOEUF/F DAEU BAOEU DAEU FPLT

SEVN FPLT JUS TAEUK –T BOKZ BAK AO SAEUV FAEUS FPLT

AEUT FPLT –T BES TAO HOEP FOER S-A WURLD FUL –F PAES FPLT

NOTE: The "Question Mark" is written: STPH

NAOEUN FPLT HOU S-T BEUG POEUNT N-T KAEUS TAO KUM OUT STPH

TEN FPLT –T GROUND –S TAOE HARD TAO PLANT –T TRAEZ AU FLOURZ FPLT

LEVN FPLT –T FAEL TRAOGT –FT PLAEU –S AUFN LAU*S AU/LAUNG –T WAEU FPLT

TWEVL FPLT EUT TOK AUL NAOEUT LAUNG FOERT WURK TAO GET DUN FPLT

THAEN FPLT TAO FAEL SAEUF/F AO SOUND –S AUL –T LEULGTS GEURL WUNTD FPLT

FRAEN FPLT –T PLAEUN TOK AUF N-T AEUR AO SAON EUT WENT OUT –F SAOEUT FPLT

GLAEN FPLT –T LAU/SAOT MAEU KUM TAO A KOERT KAEUS N-A FAOU DAEUZ FPLT

SKAEN FPLT –T OELD MAN DROEV DOUN –T STRAET TEURND TAOT LEFT AO WENT STRAEUT FOERT HAOEU/WAEU FLT

STPAEN FPLT –T KAUS –F A POUND –F TAE –S HAOEUR THAN –T PRAOEUS –F A FAOEUN BAULGTS –F WAOEUN FPLT

AEN FPLT –T BOEUZ TOELD US P-T SAEUM LA*S NAEUM –S N-T FOEN BOK TWEVL TAOEUMZ FPLT

STPHRAEN FPLT FRENDZ –F MAOEUN KAEUM OEVR FOER A STAEUK AO BAEUKD BAENZ KOK/OUT LA*S NAOEUT FPLT

TWEU FPLT NOU S-T TAOEUM FOER AUL GOD MEN TAO KUM TAOT AEUD –F US AUL FPLT

Finally, before turning to the MASTER KEY section, let's TRANSCRIBE SENTENCES.

Take a pencil and paper – TRANSCRIBE the above SENTENCES – include all the punctuation. This section is to be done only once.

After you have read and transcribed all of the SENTENCES, turn to the MASTER KEY section and check your SENTENCES for spelling, punctuation, and correctness.

Read Part B OUT LOUD. Repeat 20 times.

1. It is quite a known fact that the state is right.

2. The whole thing came out in the middle of the store.

3. Often it is called a battle for the cause.

4. The dear little child is in the front of the house.

5. Call me and say that all the wrong is in the past.

6. Each man is to take life day by day.

7. Just take the books back and save face.

8. The best to hope for is a world full of peace.

9. How is the big point in the case to come out?

10. The ground is too hard to plant the trees and flowers.

11. The real truth of the lay is often lost along the way.

12. It took all night long for the work to get done.

13. To feel safe and sound is all the little girl wanted.

14. The plane took off in the air and soon it went out of sight.

15. The lawsuit may come to a court case in a few days.

16. The old man drove down the street, turned to the left, and went straight for the highway.

17. The cost of a pound of tea is higher than the price of a fine bottle of wine.

18. The boys told us that the same last name is in the phone book twelve times.

19. Friends of mine came over for a steak and baked beans cookout last night.

20. Now is the time for all good men to come to the aid of us all.

C. Now, let's WRITE SENTENCES.

Write each SENTENCE beginning with the NUMBER, followed by a "Period." End each SENTENCE with the proper punctuation, which will usually be a "Period."

At this stage of your writing, you will NOT be writing any punctuation within the SENTENCE, such as the "Comma." Your only concern is to write what the Speaker has said.

Use this simple procedure for all the WRITE SENTENCES sections.

After you have written all the SENTENCES, please turn to the MASTER KEY section and check you outlines.

1. Great men come to show us that life is full of good.

2. It is now time to get up and make the best of it.

3. The little boy hit the ball all the way to the right side of the field and made it to first base.

4. To buy the wheat and flour at that price is part of the terms.

5. Is that the best way to clean mud and dirt off shoes?

6. The food got turned over and down it went, all over the books.

7. Less light is given to the plants in the P.M. than in the A.M.

8. The young girls told us that the school is at least four more blocks away.

9. To check the plans and list the needs of the whole town is a lot of work for just one man.

10. The rest of the boys ought to stay out of sight for now.

11. Write to me and tell me all the news of the guys in the troops.

12. The old man told me it is miles away and the name of the place is High View.

13. Get the name of the case, the date and time of the trial, and then put the files away.

14. The second time the girls saw the play, the lines seemed to make more sense.

15. Turn the lights out in the room and close the door.

16. The fair is held in the hillsides of the small town in June.

17. To force the truth out of the old man seems like a hard job.

18. The price of the car in the lot is higher than the one in the showroom.

19. My feet hurt, my back aches, and my head feels like it weighs a ton.

20. The eyes of the young girl held the look of love.

Read your notes OUT LOUD. Repeat 20 times.

NOTE: When the word "is" stands alone, it may be written with either the INITIAL S or the FINAL S.

When the word "that" stands alone, it may be written with either the INITIAL P or the FINAL P.

WUN FPLT GRAEUT MEN KUM TAO SHOE US –P LAOEUF/F –S FUL –F GOD FPLT

TO FPLT T-S NOU TAOEUM TAO GET UP AO MAEUK –T BES –F EUT FPLT

THRE FPLT –T LEULGTS BOEU HEUT –T BAUL AUL –T WAEU TAOL RAOEUT SAOEUD –FT FAELD AO MAEUD EUT TAO FEURS BAEUS FPLT

FOR FPLT TAO BAOEU –T WHAET AO FLOUR AT –T PRAOEUS –S PART –FT TEURMZ FPLT

FAOEUV FPLT S-P –T BES WAEU TAO KLAEN MUD AO DEURT AUF SHAOZ STPH

SEUX FPLT –T FAOD GAUT TEURND OEVR AO DOUN EUT WENT AUL OEVR –T BOKZ FPLT

SEVN FPLT LES LAOEUT –S GEUVN TAOT PLANTS N-T P-M THAN N-T A-M FPLT

AEUT FPLT –T YUNG GEURLZ TOELD US P-T SKUL –S AT LAE*S FOR MOER BLAUKS AU/WAEU FPLT

NAOEUN FPLT TAO KHEK –T PLANZ AO LEUS –T NAEDZ –FT HOEL TOUN S-A LAUT –F WURK FOER JUS WUN MAN FPLT

TEN FPLT –T RES –FT BOEUZ AUT TAO STAEU OUT –F SAOEUT FOER NOU FPLT

LEVN FPLT RAOEUT TAO MAE AO TEL MAE AUL –T NAOZ –FT GAOEUZ N-T TRAOPS FPLT

TWEVL FPLT –T OELD MAN TOELD MAE T-S MAOEULZ AU/WAEU AO-T NAEUM –FT PLAEUS –S HAOEU VAOU SKWR-RBGS FPLT

THAEN FPLT GET –T NAEUM –FT KAEUS –T DAEUT AO TAOEUM –FT TRAOEUL AO THEN POT –T FAOEULZ AU/WAEU FPLT

FRAEN FPLT –T SEKD TAOEUM –T GEURLZ SAU –T PLAEU –T LAOEUNZ SAEUMD TAO MAEUK MOER SENS FPLT

GLAEN FPLT TEURN –T LAOEUTS OUT N-T RAOM AO KLOEZ –T DOER FPLT

SKAEN FPLT –T FAEUR –S HELD N-T HEUL/SAOEUDZ –FT SMAUL TOUN N- JAON SKWR-RBGS FPLT

STPAEN FPLT TAO FOERS –T TRAOGT OUT –FT OELD MAN SAEMZ LAOEUK A HARD JAUB FPLT

AEN FPLT –T PRAOEUS –FT KA N-T LAUT –S HAOEUR THAN –T WUN N-T SHOE/RAOM FPLT

STPHRAEN FPLT MAOEU FAET HEURT MAOEU BAK AEUKZ AO MAOEU HED FAELZ LAOEUK EUT WAEUZ A TUN FPLT

TWEU FPLT –T AOEUZ –FT YUNG GEURL HELD –T LOK –F LUV FPLT

JURY CHARGE #1 – BRIEF AND PHRASES

To achieve the status of RPR, which signifi8es Registered Professional Reporter, a test is given by the National Shorthand Reporters Association. This test is given twice a year; once in May and once in November.

The test consists of two parts:

1. Written Knowledge Test (WKT)
2. Machine Shorthand Tests

Simply stated: The WKT is a test of the student's knowledge of the "academics" of the profession such as legal and medical terminology, transcription, and English.

The Machine Shorthand Tests are the actual "speed-writing" sections.

The machine portion consists of three categories:

1. Literary
2. Jury Charge
3. Q & A (Testimony)

A five minute test is given in each category at the following speeds:

1. Literary – 180 wpm
2. Jury Charge – 200 wpm
3. Q & A (Testimony) – 225 wpm

The above speeds represent "Reporting" status. Strive for perfection to obtain them. This is your final goal.

Now, it is time to learn to write JURY CHARGE material.

What is a JURY CHARGE?

Simply stated: A JURY CHARGE or Judge's Charge is a "charge to the jury" by the Court of a set of instructions that must be followed in this particular case, based upon the evidence produced at trial and the applicable laws.

These instructions are given at the end of the case.

JURY CHARGE material can be very repetitive in nature simply because the same instructions apply from one case to another.

The proper way to study the following JURY CHARGE will be:

1. READ each word of the JURY CHARGE in Section A, paying special attention to the new Briefs and Phrases -- 5 times.

2. WRITE the JURY CHARGE in Section B -- 5 times; and READ your notes each time.

3. WRITE the JURY CHARGE in Section B -- 1 final time and use this "Perfect Outline Stenoprint Notes" for reading practice; READ your notes -- 10 times.

Here are the new BRIEFS AND PHRASES that will appear in JURY CHARGE #1. Derivatives will also be listed where applicable, for ease in learning.

WORD	WRITTEN
Ladies and Gentlemen of the Jury	LAEUDZ/JEJ
follow	FOL
consider	K-R
consideration	K-RGS
instruct	STRUKT
instruction	STRUKGS
duty	DAOUT
also	-LS
determine	DERM
determination	DERM/AEUGS
evidence	EV
evident	EVT
produce	PRAO

about	B-
influence	FLU
sympathy	SEUGT
prejudice	PREJ
judge	J-
judgment	J-MT
regard	RARD
however	HOUVR
after	AFR
apply	PLEU
applicable	PLEUBL
together	TOEGT
as you have	ZUV
decide	SDAOEUD (Inverted "DS")
decision	SDEUGS (Inverted "DS")
these	THAEZ

A. Now, let's READ JURY CHARGE #1. (All new BRIEFS AND PHRASES are underlined.)

LAEUDZ/JEJ EUL NOU TEL U SUM -FT RULZ U MUS <u>FOL</u> N- <u>K-R</u>/-G TH- KAEUS FPLT EUL <u>STRUKT</u> U OT LAU FPLT T-S UR <u>DAOUT</u> TAO <u>FOL</u> -T LAU FPLT T-S <u>-LS</u> UR <u>DAOUT</u> TAO <u>DERM</u> -T FAKZ FPLT U MUS <u>DERM</u> -T FAKZ ONL FR-T <u>EV</u> <u>PRAOD</u> N- KOERT FPLT U SHON GES <u>B-</u> NEU FAK FPLT U MUS -N -B <u>FLUD</u> BAOEU <u>SEUGT</u> OER <u>PREJ</u> FPLT U -R -T DOEL <u>J-Z</u> -FT FAKZ FPLT U MUS TAEUK AU/KOUNT -F AUL MAOEU <u>STRUKGSZ</u> OT LAU FPLT U -R -N TAO PEUK OUT WUN <u>STRUKGS</u> OER PART -F WUN AO DEUS/<u>RARD</u> -T UGTS FPLT <u>HOUVR</u> <u>AFR</u> UV <u>DERMD</u> -T FAKZ U MAEU FAOEUND -P SUM <u>STRUKGSZ</u> DAON <u>PLEU</u> FPLT U MUS THEN <u>K-R</u> -T STRUKGSZ -P DAO <u>PLEU</u> <u>TOEGT</u> W-T FAKZ <u>ZUV</u> <u>DERMD</u> THEM FPLT <u>SDAOEUD</u> -T KAEUS BAOEU <u>PLEUG</u> -T LAU N- <u>THAEZ</u> <u>STRUKGSZ</u> TAOT FAKZ FPLT

B. Now, let's WRITE JURY CHARGE #1. (All new BRIEFS AND PHRASES are underlined.)

<u>Ladies and Gentlemen of the Jury</u>:

I will now tell you some of the rules you must <u>follow</u> in <u>consider</u>ing this case. I will <u>instruct</u> you on the law. It is your <u>duty</u> to <u>follow</u> the law.

It is <u>also</u> your <u>duty</u> to <u>determine</u> the facts. You must <u>determine</u> the facts only from the <u>evidence</u> <u>produced</u> in court. You should not guess <u>about</u> any fact. You must not be <u>influence</u>d by <u>sympathy</u> or <u>prejudice</u>.

You are the sole <u>judges</u> of the facts.

You must take account of all my <u>instructions</u> on the law. You are not to pick out one <u>instruction</u> or part of one and dis<u>regard</u> the others. <u>However</u>, <u>after</u> you have <u>determined</u> the facts, you may find that some <u>instructions</u> do not <u>apply</u>. You must then <u>consider</u> the <u>instructions</u> that do <u>apply</u>, <u>together</u> with the facts <u>as you have determined</u> them. <u>Decide</u> the case by <u>apply</u>ing the law in <u>these instructions</u> to the facts.

C. This section will contain a list of ten (10) new BRIEFS and ten (10) new PHRASES.

BRIEFS	WRITTEN
abdomen	ABD
above	BUV (Conflict "buff" – very infrequent court word)
absolute	SLAOT
accept	SEP
accident	SDENT
accomplish	PLEUSH
acknowledge	AK/-J
actual	ACH
address	DREUS
advance	VANS

PHRASES	WRITTEN
accident happened	SDAPD
accident occurred	SDURD
all right	L-RT
are you married	RUMD
as a matter of fact	ZMAFT
as a result	ZARLT
as the result	ZERLT
as long as	Z-LGZ
ask you	SK-U (SK = "ask)
ask your	SK-UR (SK = "ask)

Read your notes OUT LOUD. Repeat 20 times.

The following sentences contain the new BRIEFS AND PHRASES of Section C. As you practice writing, read each sentence OUT LOUD. All new BRIEFS AND PHRASES are underlined.

1. <u>As long as</u> you're going to the store, will you please get me a change of <u>address</u> card?

2. When the <u>accident happened</u>, I had no <u>actual</u> fear of danger.

3. <u>As a result</u> of all his hard studying, he was able to <u>accomplish</u> his goal.

4. Her pain was just <u>above</u> the <u>abdomen</u>.

5. <u>As a matter of fact</u>, I need you to <u>ask your</u> boss about the new job.

6. <u>All right</u>, <u>are you married</u> or single?

7. Please <u>acknowledge</u> that the <u>advance</u> classes will be taught this fall.

8. When the <u>accident occurred</u>, did you <u>accept</u> any ticket?

9. <u>As the result</u> of testing, we now have <u>absolute</u> proof it will work.

10. I would like to <u>ask you</u> about the <u>accident</u> if you are not too busy.

Read your notes OUT LOUD. Repeat 20 times.

www.ingramcontent.com/pod-product-compliance
Lightning Source LLC
Chambersburg PA
CBHW082206300426

44117CB00016B/2687